THE THINKING TREE BOOK OF STATE FLOWERS

Nature Study Handbook

Learning about the botanical flowers for all 50 US States, locating their scientific names, research projects, creative activities, and more!

Written and Designed by:
Nora McCain Apple

Illustrations/Artwork by: Anna Kidalova
Cover Artwork by: Sarah Janisse Brown

FunSchooling.com

The Thinking Tree, LLC

Dyslexie© Font by: *Christian Boer*

My name is: ____________________
____
Date: ____________________________
Age: ________________

Instructions:

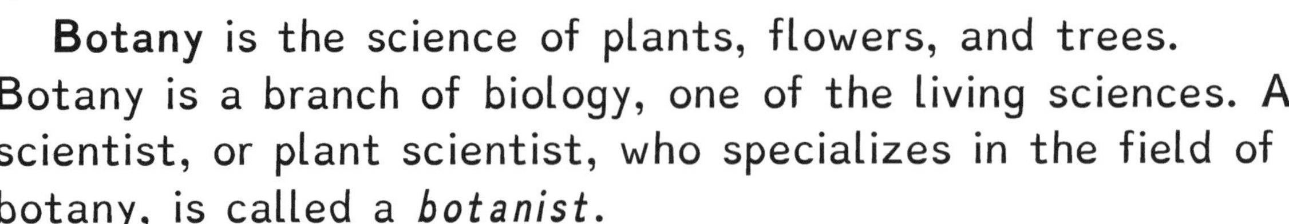

Botany is the science of plants, flowers, and trees. Botany is a branch of biology, one of the living sciences. A scientist, or plant scientist, who specializes in the field of botany, is called a *botanist*.

Humans began studying plants as far back as Adam and Eve. It was necessary to identify which plants were edible or poisonous, and which plants could be used for medicine. Today, botanists study approximately **410,000** species of plants!

This workbook will include science, geography, history, language arts, and creative arts all in one! If you are using the book for school, work on one page a day, or as many as you want to fit into your curriculum. The vocabulary words are located at the beginning so you will understand the terms when you research each state flower.

This is a workbook purposed to develop research skills. Think of all the different ways to research the flower species. Use a dictionary in book form to look up and learn the vocabulary words. Have your parent help with any searches on the Internet or schedule a library day to research the information. Choose your favorite reading spot, such as a beanbag chair, comfy desk, or under your favorite oak tree. Be sure to have colored pencils, pens, or markers ready to doodle and practice your art skills!

I know you will have fun learning about our amazing botanical earth!

UNITED STATES OF AMERICA

Find and color your state!

What State do you live in? ______________________________

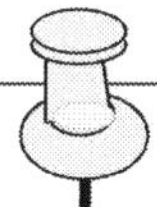

Here are some helpful websites for your parents to help with your research:

- https://www.50states.com/flower/
- https://state.1keydata.com/state-flowers.php
- https://statesymbolsusa.org/categories/flower
- https://en.wikipedia.org/wiki/List_of_U.S._state_and_territory_flowers
- https://www.usbg.gov/gardens/rare-and-endangered-plants-gallery

VOCABULARY WORDS

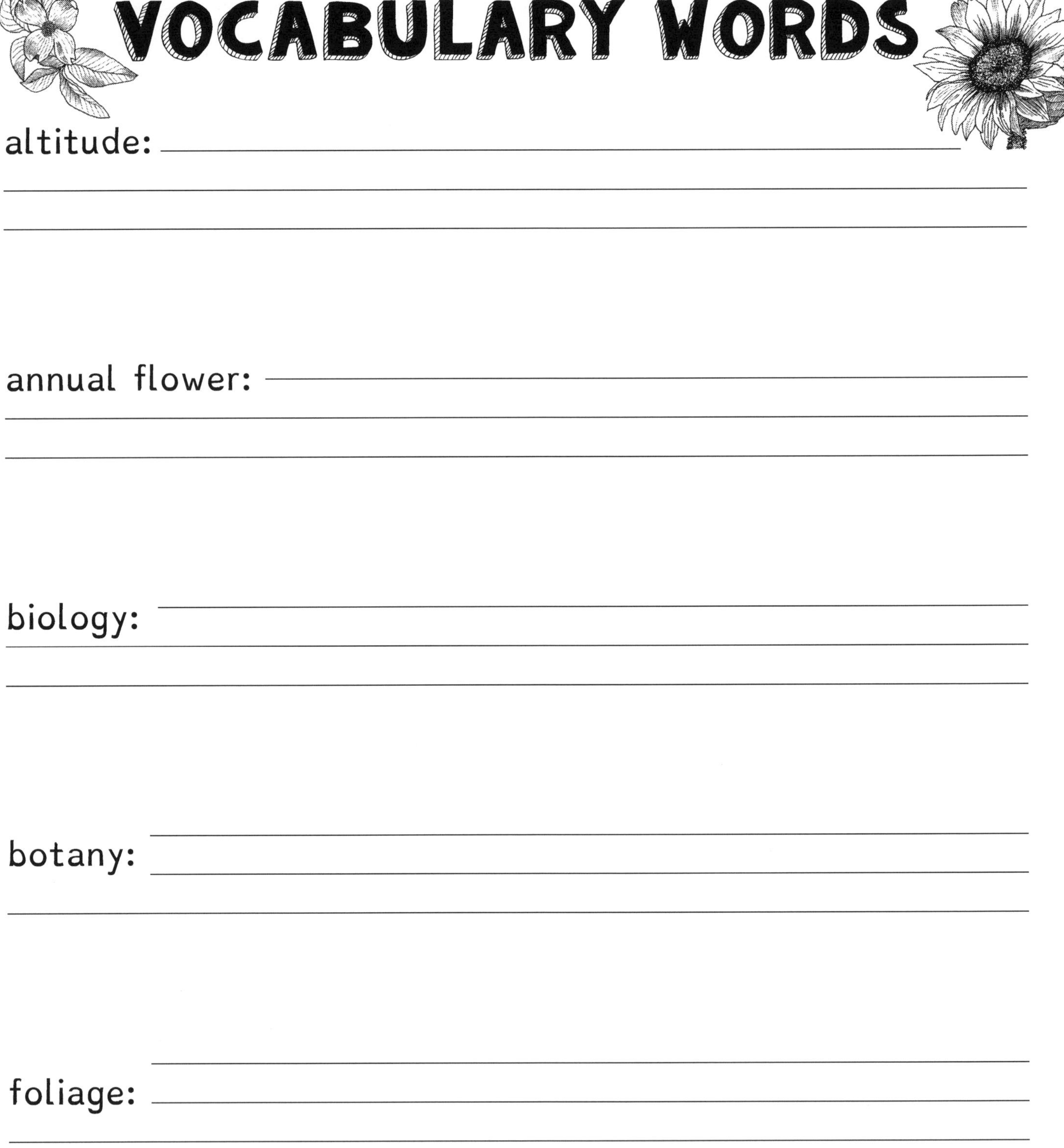

altitude: ______________________________

annual flower: ______________________________

biology: ______________________________

botany: ______________________________

foliage: ______________________________

geography: ______________________________

VOCABULARY WORDS

organic matter:

perennial flower:

poisonous plant:

science:

soil:

terrain:

ALABAMA

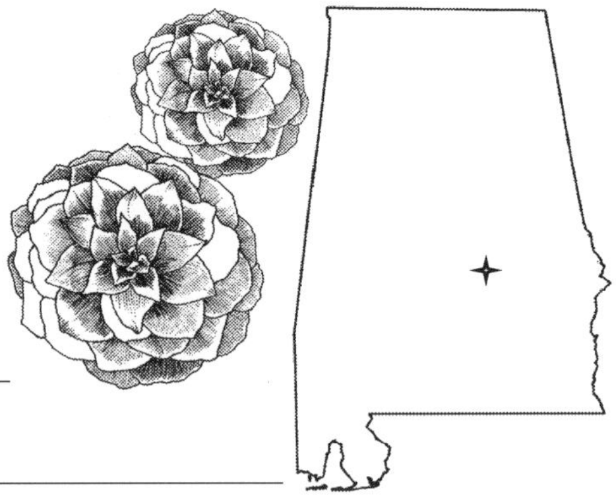

The state flower is: **Camellia**

Find the botanical name: ________________

How did this flower get its name? ________________

____

Is this flower an annual or perennial? ________________

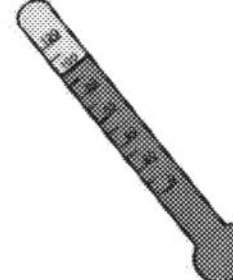

What range in temperature is best for this flower?
High: __________ Low: __________

How many hours of daily sunlight are needed for this flower? ______

Does this flower grow best in high or low altitude? ________

List the type(s) of soil needed to grow the state flower: ________

____

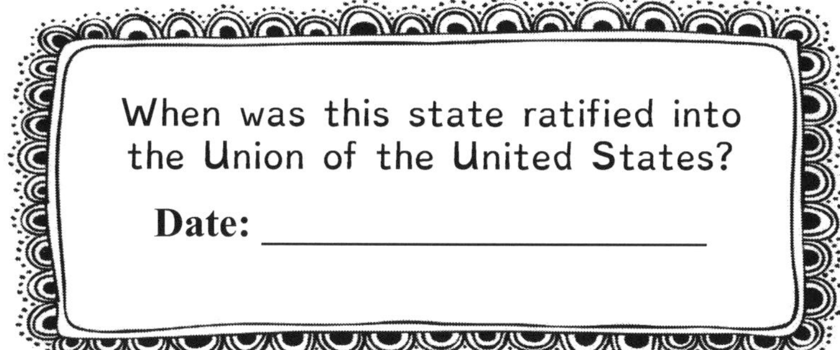

CREATIVE WRITING

In the space below, write a poem, short story, or a unique history tid-bit about the state flower. If this flower is in your state, and in bloom, try taping one to this page and press it in the book!

____

____

____

____

____

____

____

Which country did this flower originate?

____

List the different colors of this flower:

____

____

____

List the sources you used to research this flower:

Books: ____

____

Websites: ____

____

Other sources: ____

____

ALASKA

The state flower is: **Forget-me-not**

Find the botanical name: ____________________

How did this flower get its name? ______________________________

Is this flower an annual or perennial? __________________

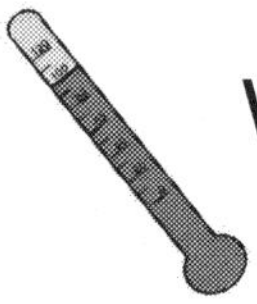

What range in temperature is best for this flower?
High: __________ Low: ____________

How many hours of daily sunlight are needed for this flower? ______

Does this flower grow best in high or low altitude? __________

List the type(s) of soil needed to grow the state flower: ________

____

Fun fact:
Forget-me-nots are found throughout the Himalaya Mountains at elevations of 9,800–14,100 feet (3,000–4,300 meters).

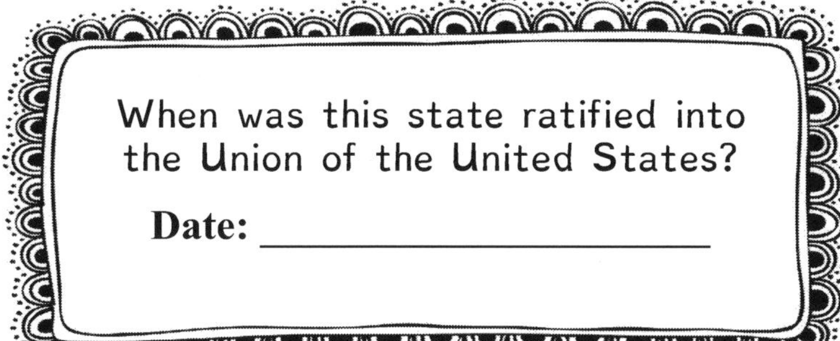

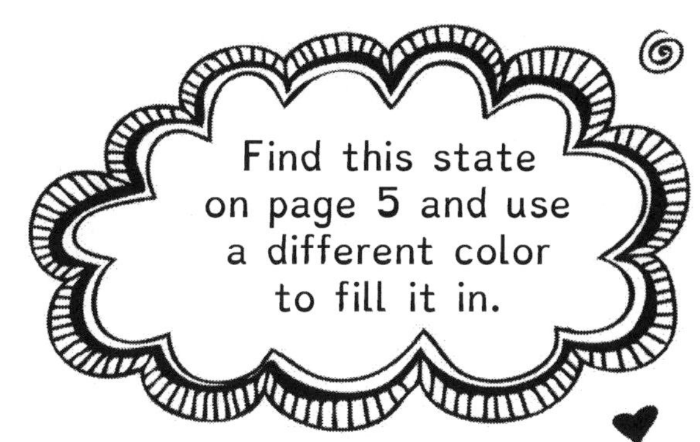

CREATIVE WRITING

In the space below, write a poem, short story, or a unique history tid-bit about the state flower. If this flower is in your state, and in bloom, try taping one to this page and press it in the book!

____

____

____

____

____

____

____

Which country did this flower originate?

____

List the different colors of this flower:

____

____

____

List the sources you used to research this flower:

Books: ____________________

____

Websites: ____________________

____

Other sources: ____________________

____

ARIZONA

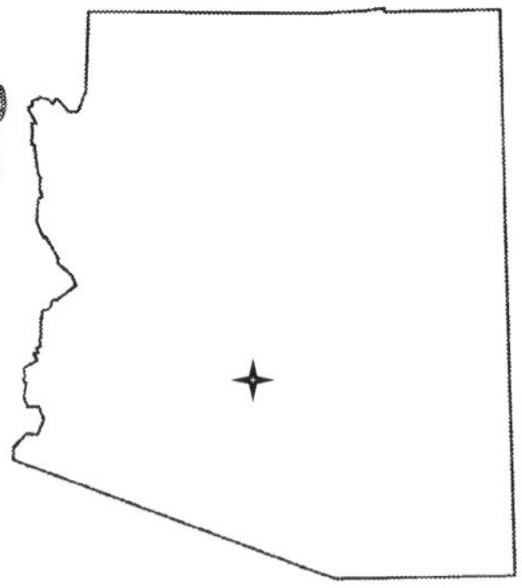

The state flower is:

Saguaro Cactus Blossom

Find the botanical name: ____________________

How did this flower get its name? ______________________________

____

Is this flower an annual or perennial? __________________

What range in temperature is best for this flower?

High: __________ Low: ____________

How many hours of daily sunlight are needed for this flower? ______

Does this flower grow best in high or low altitude? ____________

List the type(s) of soil needed to grow the state flower: _________

____

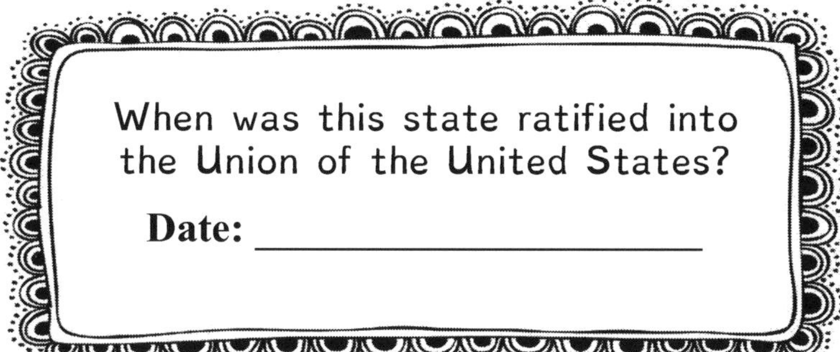

When was this state ratified into the Union of the United States?

Date: ____________________

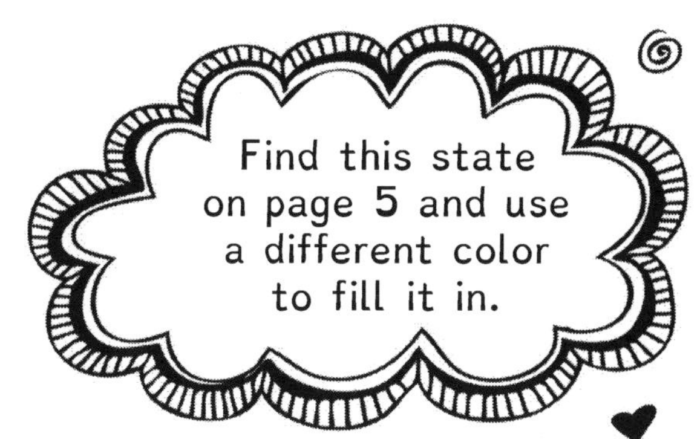

Find this state on page 5 and use a different color to fill it in.

CREATIVE WRITING

In the space below, write a poem, short story, or a unique history tid-bit about the state flower. If this flower is in your state, and in bloom, try taping one to this page and press it in the book!

____

____

____

____

____

____

____

Which country did this flower originate?

____

List the different colors of this flower:

____

____

____

List the sources you used to research this flower:

Books: ____

____

Websites: ____

____

Other sources: ____

____

ARKANSAS

The state flower is: **Apple Blossom**

Find the botanical name: ____________________

How did this flower get its name? ______________________________

____

Is this flower an annual or perennial? __________________

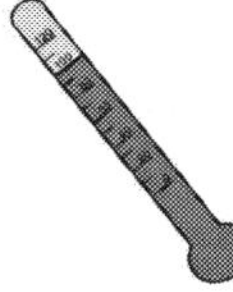

What range in temperature is best for this flower?
High: ___________ Low: ____________

How many hours of daily sunlight are needed for this flower? ______

Does this flower grow best in high or low altitude? _________

List the type(s) of soil needed to grow the state flower: _________

____

Interesting fact: The Apple Blossom was chosen as the state flower of Arkansas in 1901, when the state was one of the largest apple producers in the U.S. Then, in 1927, the crops were damaged by disease and severe frost. Apple production plummeted, today ranking Arkansas 32nd in production.

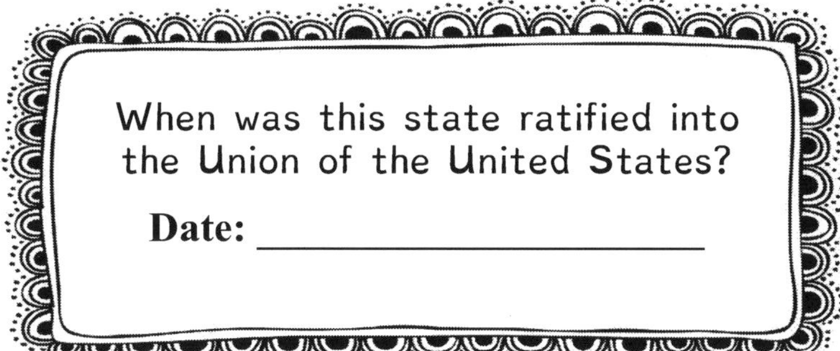

CREATIVE WRITING

In the space below, write a poem, short story, or a unique history tid-bit about the state flower. If this flower is in your state, and in bloom, try taping one to this page and press it in the book!

____

____

____

____

____

____

____

Which country did this flower originate?

____

List the different colors of this flower:

____

____

____

List the sources you used to research this flower:

Books: ____

____

Websites: ____

____

Other sources: ____

____

CALIFORNIA

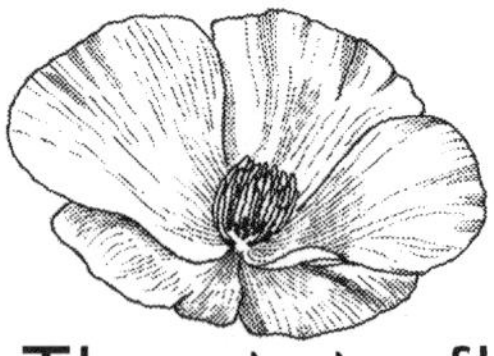

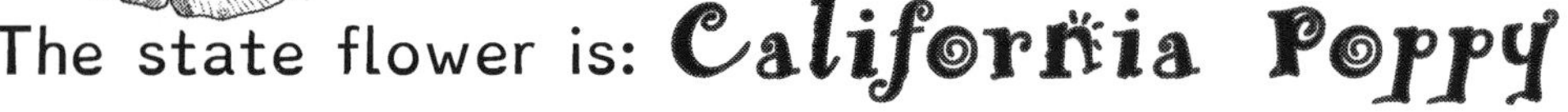

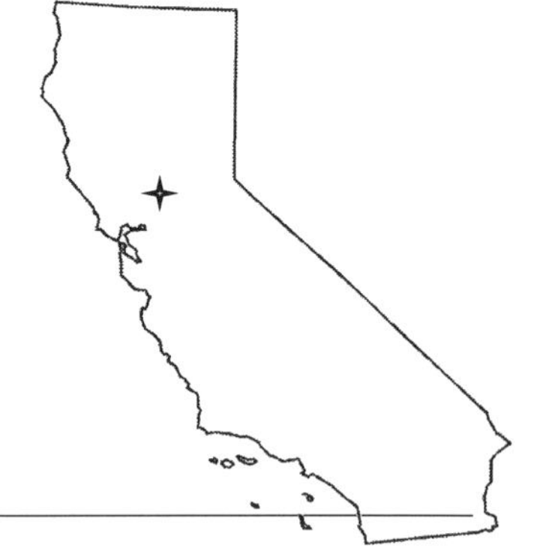

The state flower is: **California Poppy**

Find the botanical name: ____________________

How did this flower get its name? ______________________________

____

Is this flower an annual or perennial? ________________

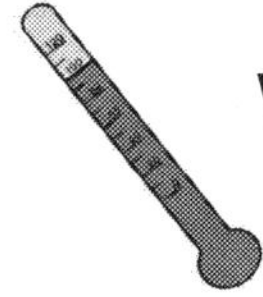

What range in temperature is best for this flower?

High: __________ Low: ____________

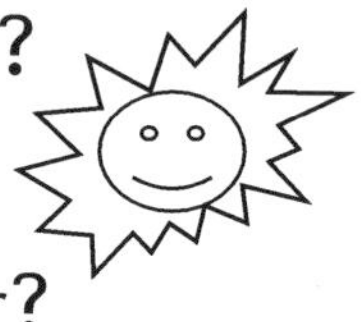

How many hours of daily sunlight are needed for this flower? ______

Does this flower grow best in high or low altitude? ___________

List the type(s) of soil needed to grow the state flower: _________

____

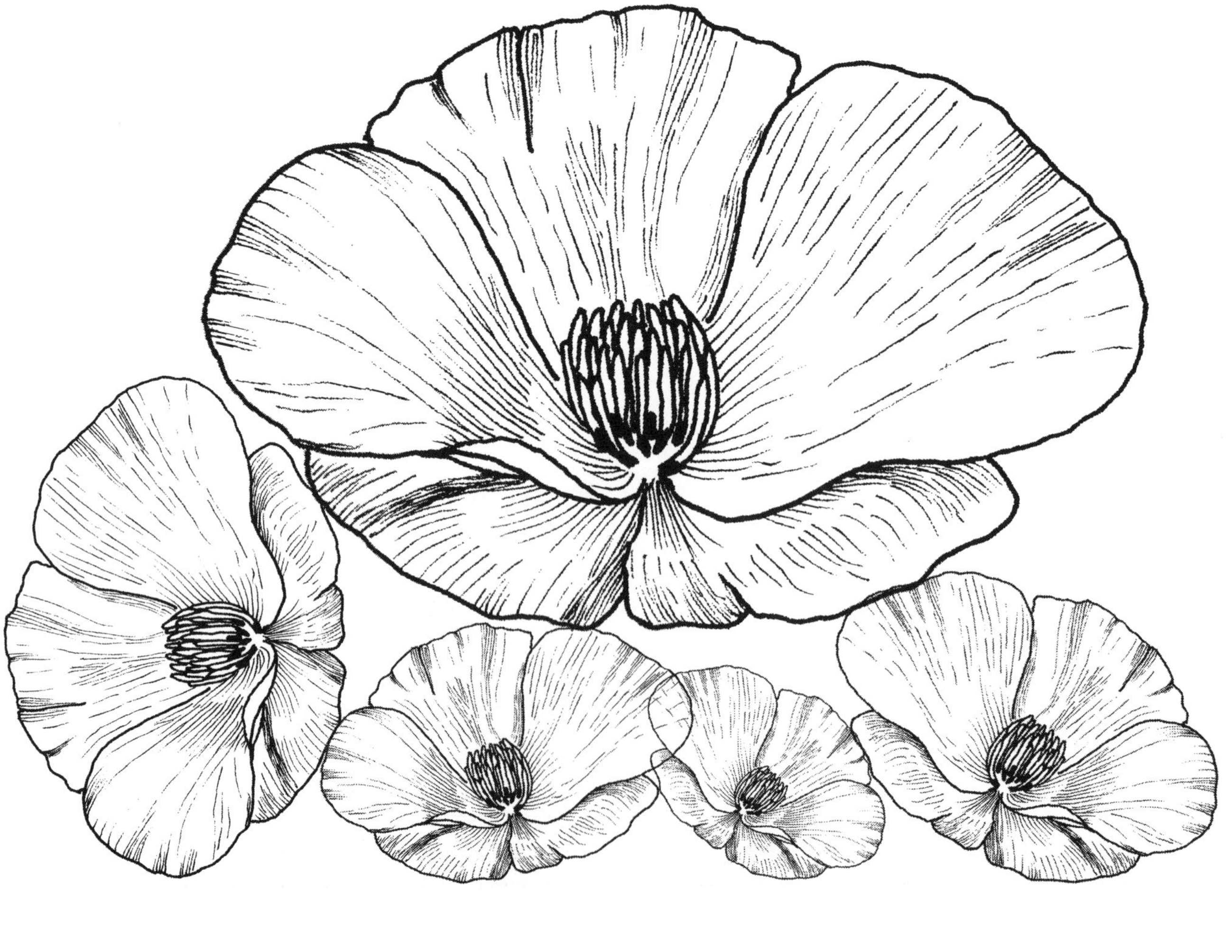

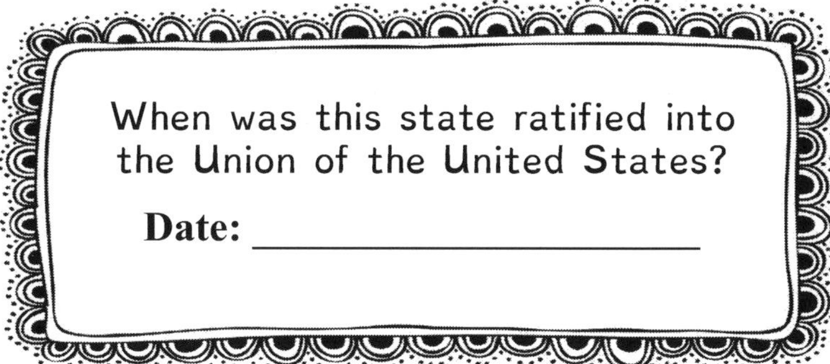

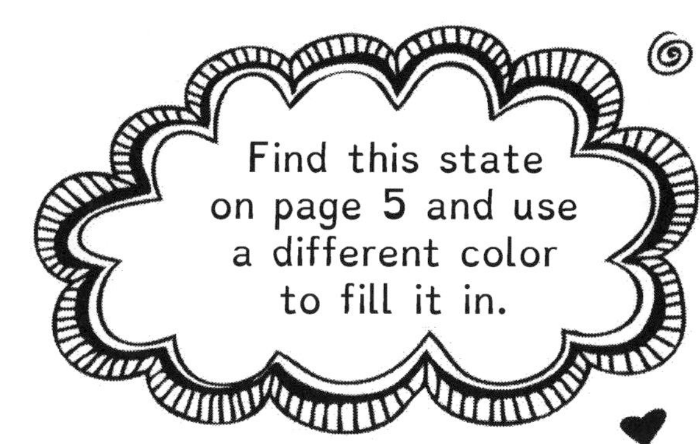

CREATIVE WRITING

In the space below, write a poem, short story, or a unique history tid-bit about the state flower. If this flower is in your state, and in bloom, try taping one to this page and press it in the book!

____

____

____

____

____

____

____

Which country did this flower originate?

____

List the different colors of this flower:

____

____

____

List the sources you used to research this flower:

Books: ______________________________

____

Websites: ______________________________

____

Other sources: ______________________________

____

CREATIVE ARTS

Fill in the missing parts. Write the name of each flower from this section:

CREATIVE ARTS

Draw your favorite flower from this section. Use your imagination to draw the flower in its natural habitat. Add a house, forest, or animals!

COLORADO

The state flower is:

Rocky Mountain Columbine

Find the botanical name: ____________________

How did this flower get its name? ______________________________

____

Is this flower an annual or perennial? __________________

What range in temperature is best for this flower?

High: ___________ Low: _____________

How many hours of daily sunlight are needed for this flower? _______

Does this flower grow best in high or low altitude? _____________

List the type(s) of soil needed to grow the state flower: _________

____

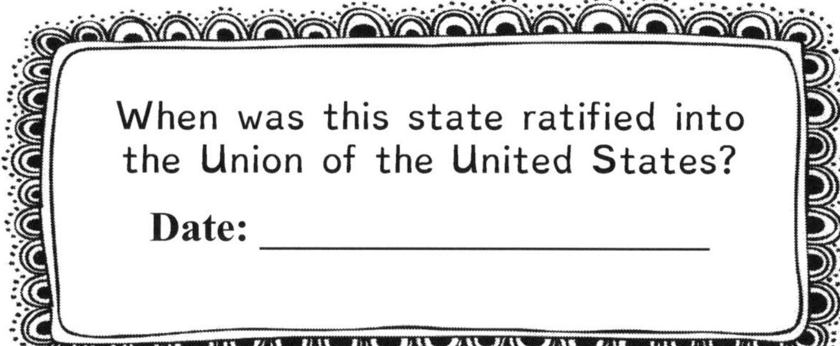

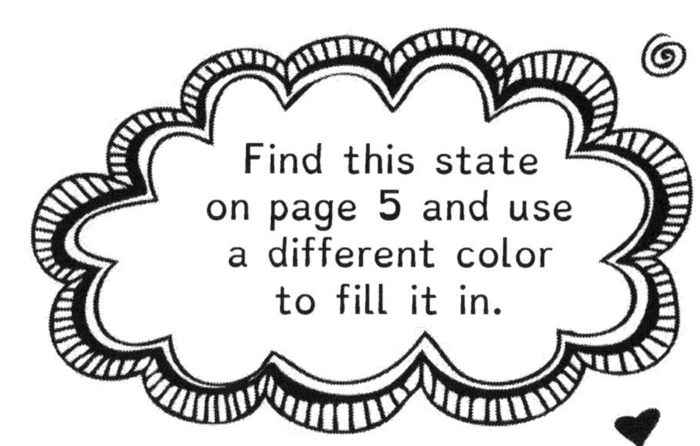

CREATIVE WRITING

In the space below, write a poem, short story, or a unique history tid-bit about the state flower. If this flower is in your state, and in bloom, try taping one to this page and press it in the book!

____

____

____

____

____

____

____

Which country did this flower originate?

____

List the different colors of this flower:

____

____

____

List the sources you used to research this flower:

Books: ____

____

Websites: ____

____

Other sources: ____

____

CONNECTICUT

The state flower is: **Mountain Laure**

Find the botanical name: ____________________

How did this flower get its name? ______________________________

____

Is this flower an annual or perennial? __________________

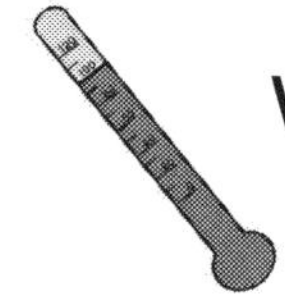

What range in temperature is best for this flower?
High: ___________ Low: _____________

How many hours of daily sunlight are needed for this flower? ______

Does this flower grow best in high or low altitude? ____________

List the type(s) of soil needed to grow the state flower: _________

____

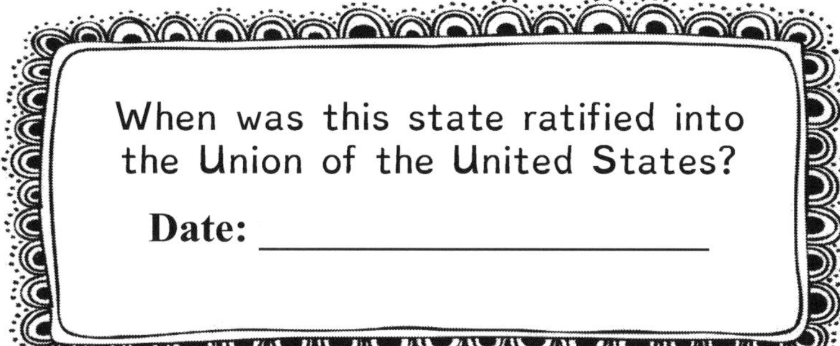

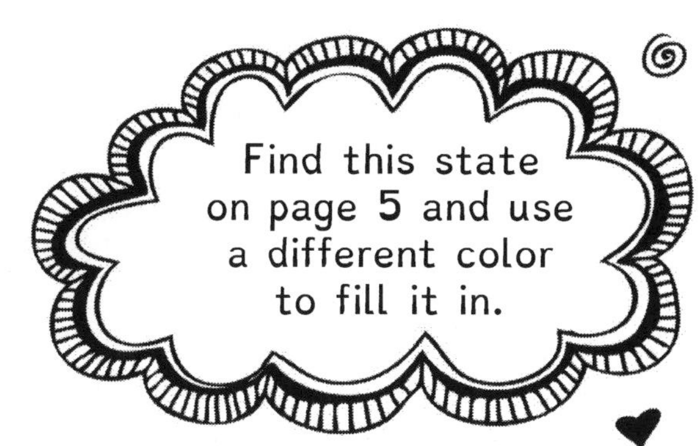

CREATIVE WRITING

In the space below, write a poem, short story, or a unique history tid-bit about the state flower. If this flower is in your state, and in bloom, try taping one to this page and press it in the book!

____

____

____

____

____

____

____

Which country did this flower originate?

____

List the different colors of this flower:

____

____

____

List the sources you used to research this flower:

Books: ____

____

Websites: ____

____

Other sources: ____

____

DELAWARE

The state flower is: **Peach Blossom**

Find the botanical name: ____________________

How did this flower get its name? ____________________

____

Is this flower an annual or perennial? ________________

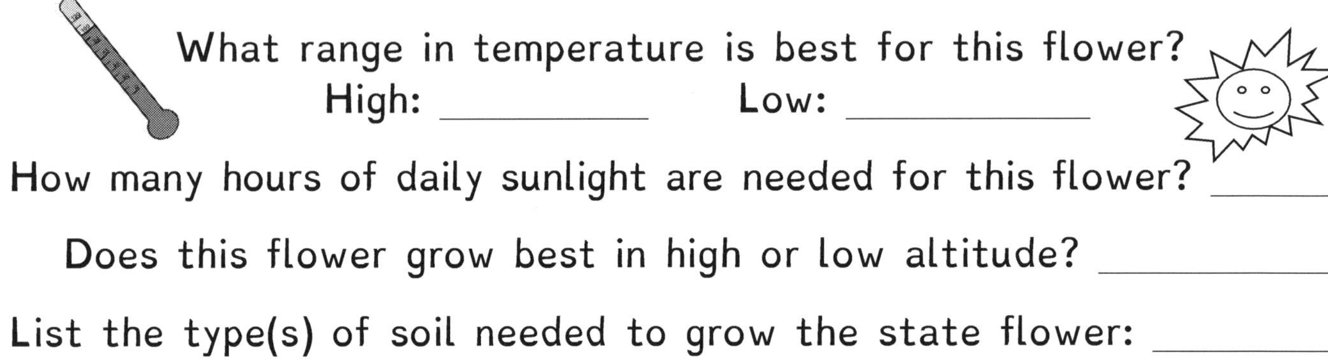

What range in temperature is best for this flower?

High: __________ Low: ____________

How many hours of daily sunlight are needed for this flower? ______

Does this flower grow best in high or low altitude? ___________

List the type(s) of soil needed to grow the state flower: ________

____

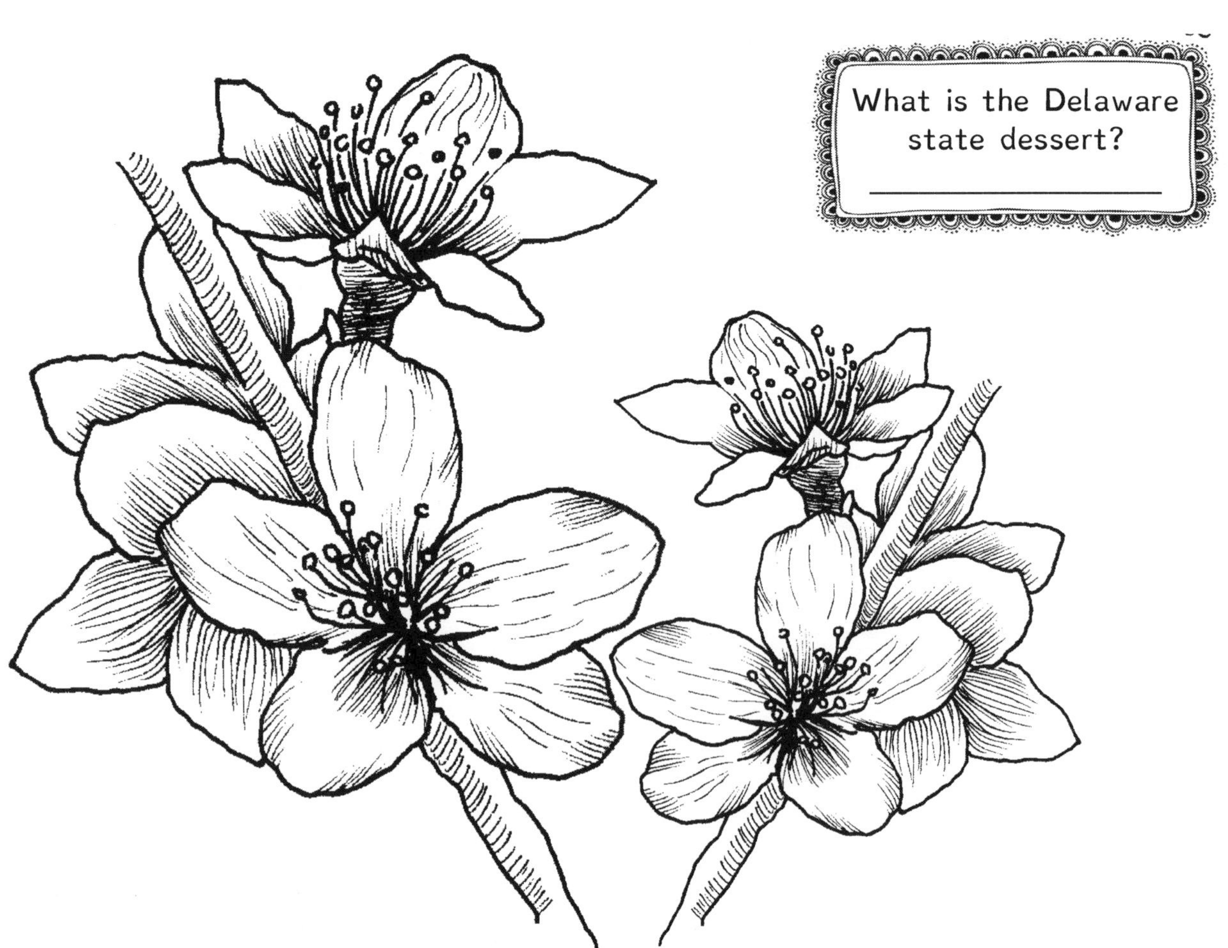

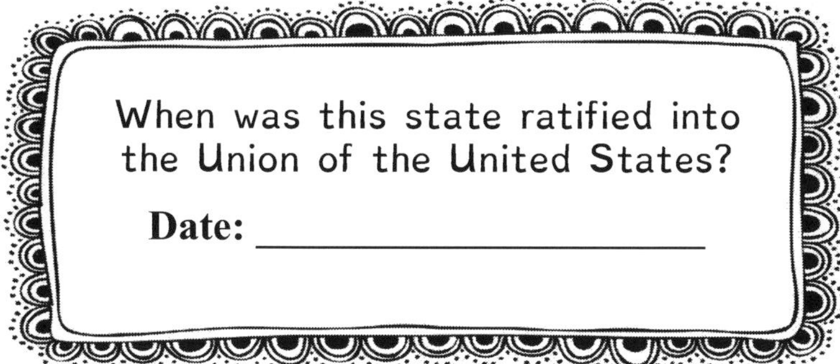

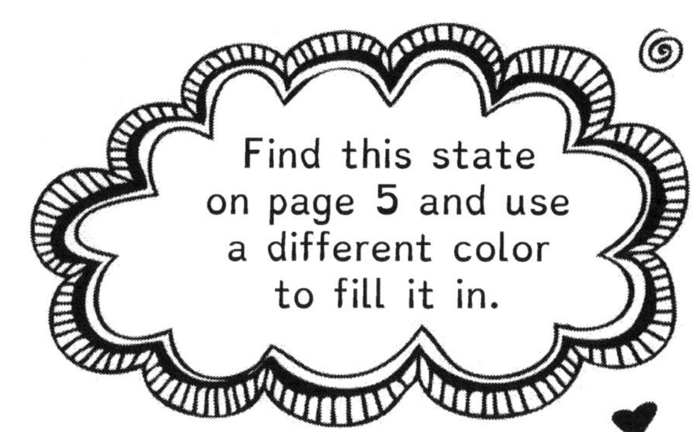

CREATIVE WRITING

In the space below, write a poem, short story, or a unique history tid-bit about the state flower. If this flower is in your state, and in bloom, try taping one to this page and press it in the book!

____

____

____

____

____

____

____

Which country did this flower originate?

____

List the different colors of this flower:

____

____

____

List the sources you used to research this flower:

Books: ____

____

Websites: ____

____

Other sources: ____

____

FLORIDA

The state flower is:

Find the botanical name: ____________________

How did this flower get its name? ______

____

Is this flower an annual or perennial? ________________

What range in temperature is best for this flower?

High: __________ Low: ____________

How many hours of daily sunlight are needed for this flower? ______

Does this flower grow best in high or low altitude? ___________

List the type(s) of soil needed to grow the state flower: _________

____

Color the oranges!

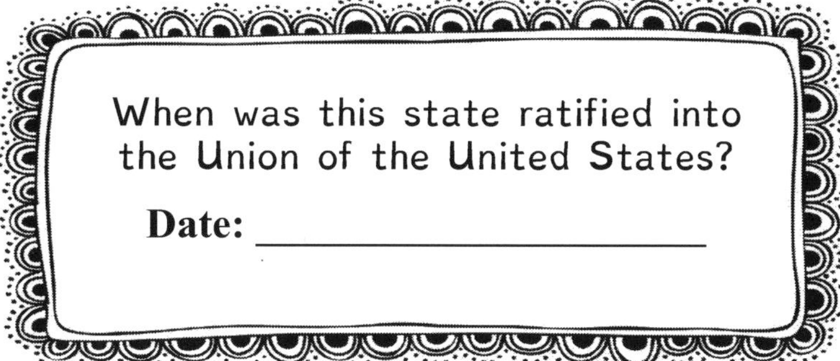

CREATIVE WRITING

In the space below, write a poem, short story, or a unique history tid-bit about the state flower. If this flower is in your state, and in bloom, try taping one to this page and press it in the book!

____

____

____

____

____

____

____

Which country did this flower originate?

____

List the different colors of this flower:

____

____

____

List the sources you used to research this flower:

Books: ____

____

Websites: ____

____

Other sources: ____

____

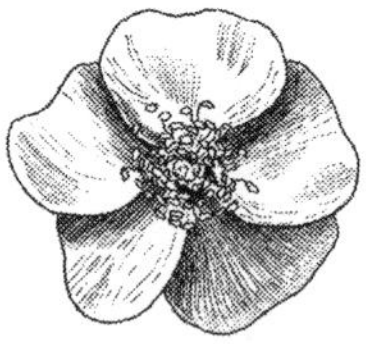

GEORGIA

The state flower is: Cherokee Rose

Find the botanical name: ___________________

How did this flower get its name? ____________

____

Is this flower an annual or perennial? ________________

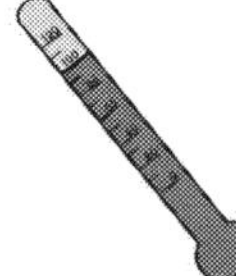

What range in temperature is best for this flower?
High: __________ Low: ____________

How many hours of daily sunlight are needed for this flower? ______

Does this flower grow best in high or low altitude? ___________

List the type(s) of soil needed to grow the state flower: ________

____

Interesting fact:
This rose represents the Trail of Tears, the forced relocation of Native Americans to the southeastern United States in the 1830's.

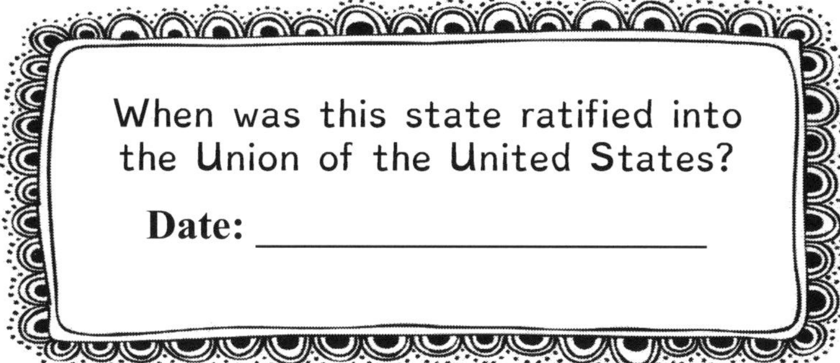

CREATIVE WRITING

In the space below, write a poem, short story, or a unique history tid-bit about the state flower. If this flower is in your state, and in bloom, try taping one to this page and press it in the book!

____

____

____

____

____

____

____

Which country did this flower originate?

____

List the different colors of this flower:

____

____

____

List the sources you used to research this flower:

Books: ____

____

Websites: ____

____

Other sources: ____

____

CREATIVE ARTS

Fill in the missing parts. Write the name of each flower from this section:

CREATIVE ARTS

Draw your favorite flower from this section. Use your imagination to draw the flower in its natural habitat. Add a house, forest, or animals!

HAWAII

The state flower is: **Hawaiian Hibiscus**

Find the botanical name: ____________________

How did this flower get its name? ______________________________

____

Is this flower an annual or perennial? __________________

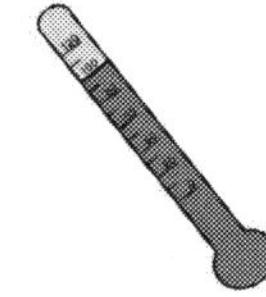

What range in temperature is best for this flower?
High: ___________ Low: _____________

How many hours of daily sunlight are needed for this flower? ______

Does this flower grow best in high or low altitude? ____________

List the type(s) of soil needed to grow the state flower: _________

____

Fun fact:
The Hibiscus is also the National flower of South Korea!

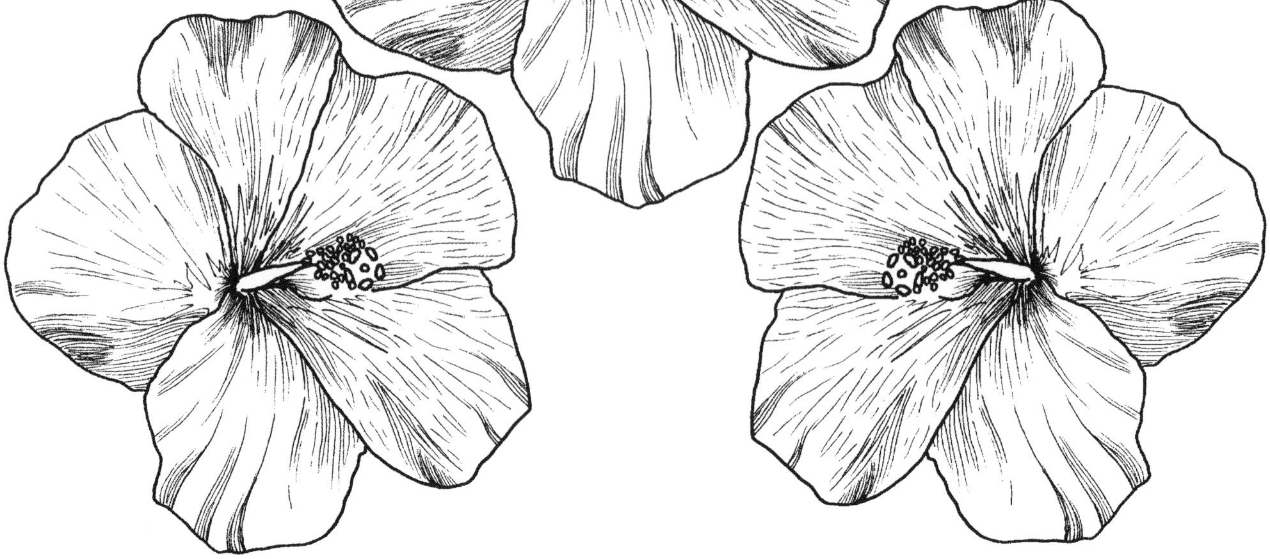

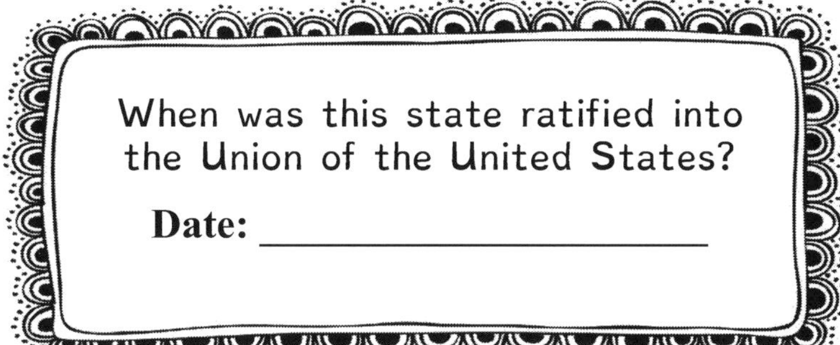

CREATIVE WRITING

In the space below, write a poem, short story, or a unique history tid-bit about the state flower. If this flower is in your state, and in bloom, try taping one to this page and press it in the book!

____

____

____

____

____

____

____

Which country did this flower originate?

____

List the different colors of this flower:

____

____

____

List the sources you used to research this flower:

Books: ____

____

Websites: ____

____

Other sources: ____

____

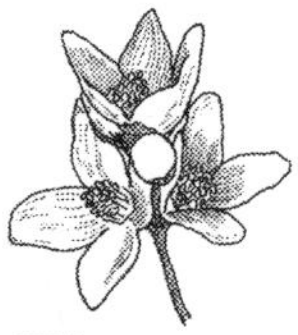

IDAHO

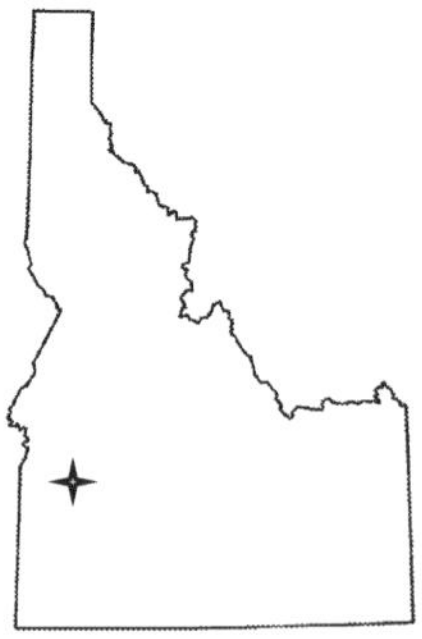

The state flower is: **Syringa Mock Orange**

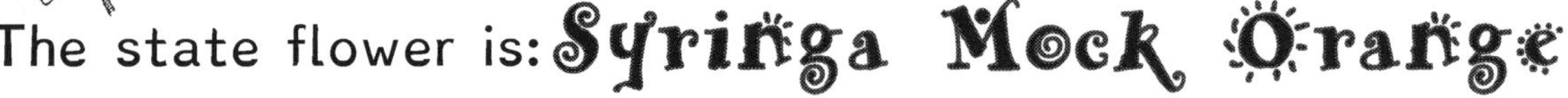

Find the botanical name: ____________________

How did this flower get its name? ______________________________

____

Is this flower an annual or perennial? __________________

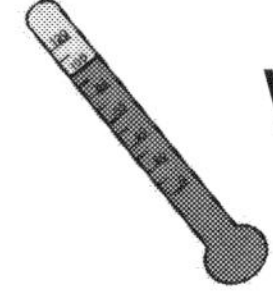

What range in temperature is best for this flower?

High: __________ Low: ____________

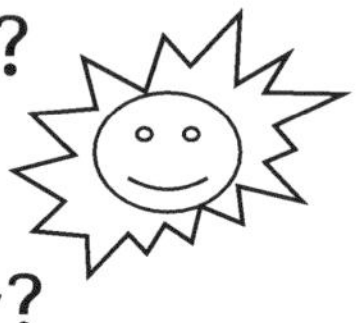

How many hours of daily sunlight are needed for this flower? ______

Does this flower grow best in high or low altitude? __________

List the type(s) of soil needed to grow the state flower: ________

____

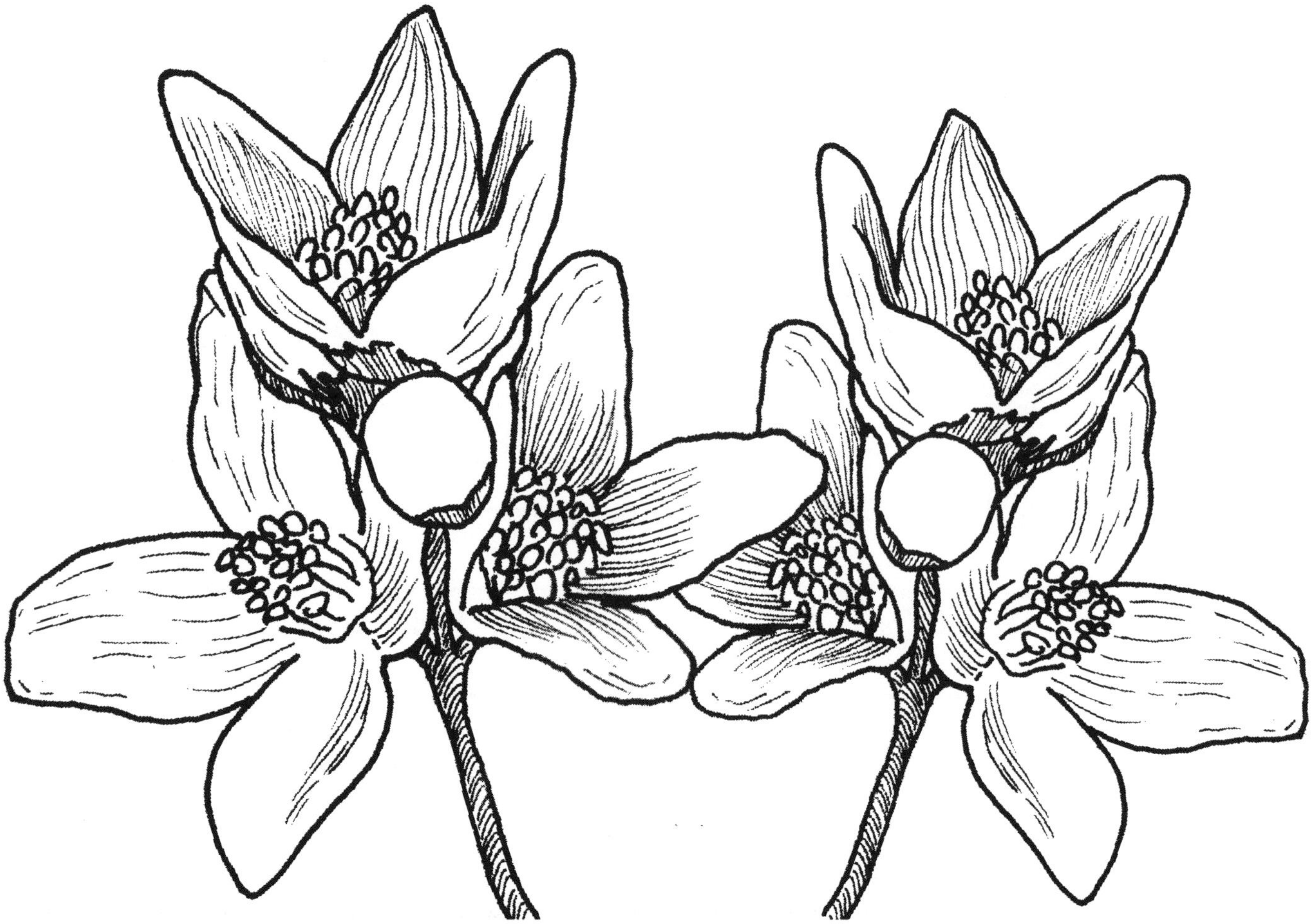

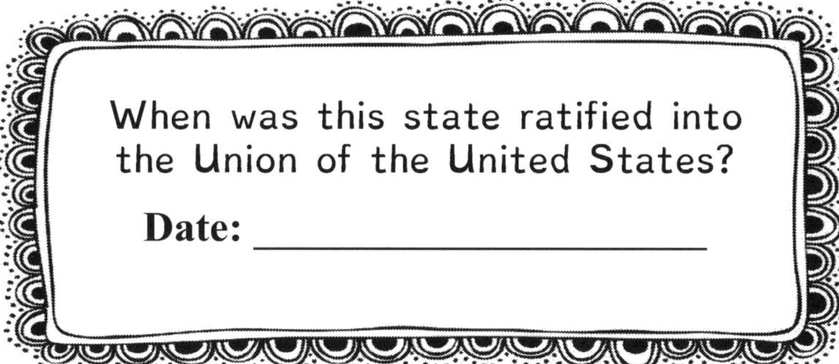

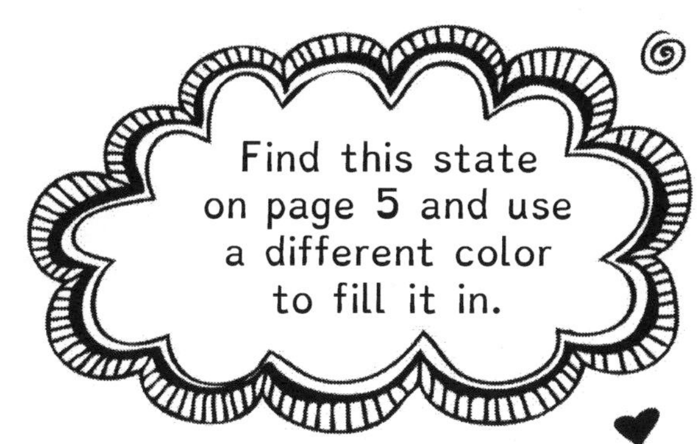

CREATIVE WRITING

In the space below, write a poem, short story, or a unique history tid-bit about the state flower. If this flower is in your state, and in bloom, try taping one to this page and press it in the book!

____

____

____

____

____

____

____

Which country did this flower originate?

____

List the different colors of this flower:

____

____

____

List the sources you used to research this flower:

Books: ____

____

Websites: ____

____

Other sources: ____

____

ILLINOIS

The state flower is: **Violet**

Find the botanical name: ____________________

How did this flower get its name? ____________________

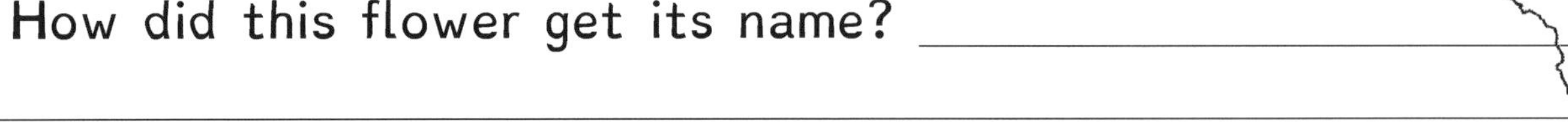

Is this flower an annual or perennial? ____________________

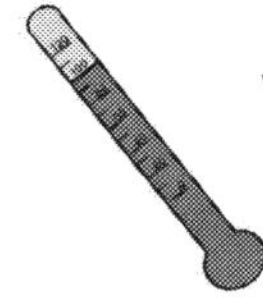

What range in temperature is best for this flower?

High: __________ Low: __________

How many hours of daily sunlight are needed for this flower? ______

Does this flower grow best in high or low altitude? __________

List the type(s) of soil needed to grow the state flower: ________

____

Fun fact:
The violet leaves and flowers are edible and used in salads and candies! The violet is also used in medicines and perfumes!

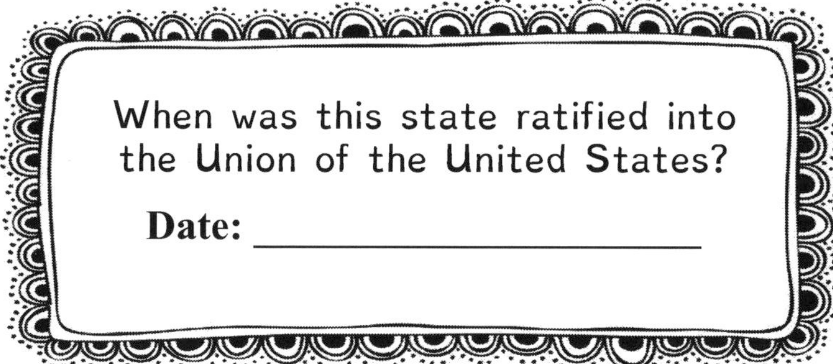

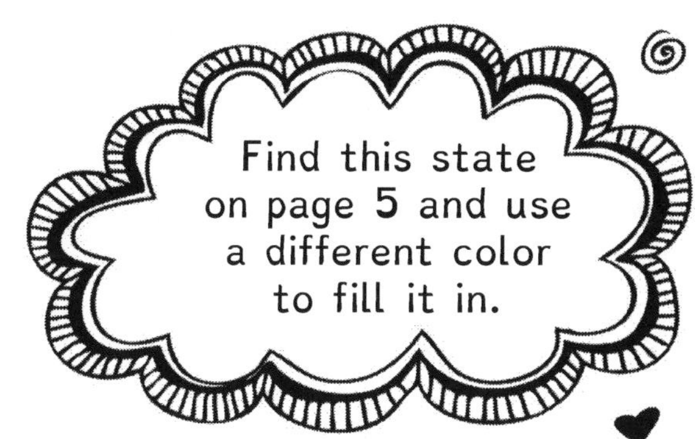

CREATIVE WRITING

In the space below, write a poem, short story, or a unique history tid-bit about the state flower. If this flower is in your state, and in bloom, try taping one to this page and press it in the book!

____

____

____

____

____

____

____

Which country did this flower originate?

____

List the different colors of this flower:

____

____

____

List the sources you used to research this flower:

Books: ____

____

Websites: ____

____

Other sources: ____________________________________

____

INDIANA

The state flower is: **Peony**

Find the botanical name: ____________________

How did this flower get its name? _________________

____

Is this flower an annual or perennial? __________________

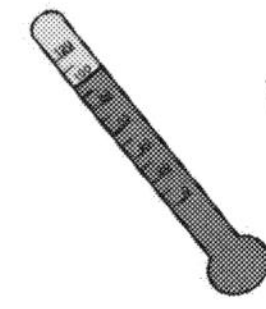

What range in temperature is best for this flower?
High: ___________ Low: _____________

How many hours of daily sunlight are needed for this flower? _______

Does this flower grow best in high or low altitude? ____________

List the type(s) of soil needed to grow the state flower: _________

____

What was the Indiana state flower from 1931 to 1957?

____

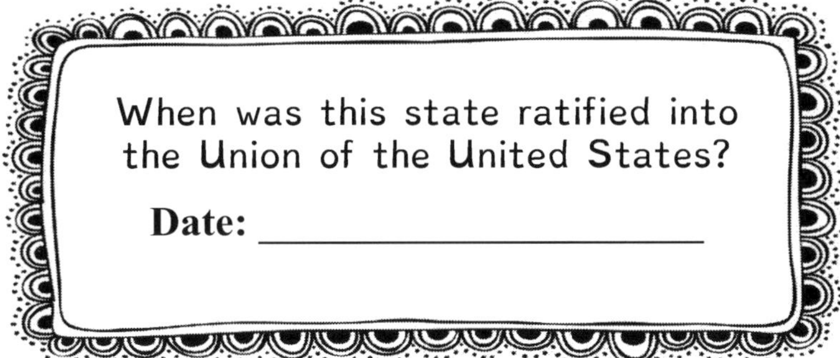

CREATIVE WRITING

In the space below, write a poem, short story, or a unique history tid-bit about the state flower. If this flower is in your state, and in bloom, try taping one to this page and press it in the book!

____

____

____

____

____

____

____

Which country did this flower originate?

____

List the different colors of this flower:

____

____

____

List the sources you used to research this flower:

Books: ____

____

Websites: ____

____

Other sources: ____

____

IOWA

The state flower is:

Wild Prairie Rose

Find the botanical name: ____________________

How did this flower get its name? ______________________________

____

Is this flower an annual or perennial? __________________

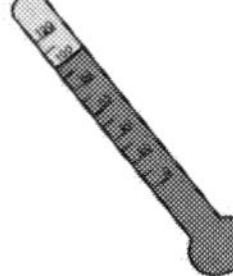

What range in temperature is best for this flower?

High: ___________ Low: _____________

How many hours of daily sunlight are needed for this flower? _______

Does this flower grow best in high or low altitude? __________

List the type(s) of soil needed to grow the state flower: _________

____

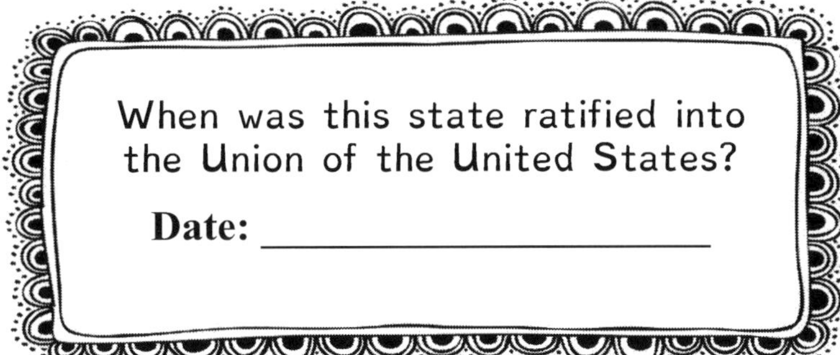

CREATIVE WRITING

In the space below, write a poem, short story, or a unique history tid-bit about the state flower. If this flower is in your state, and in bloom, try taping one to this page and press it in the book!

____

____

____

____

____

____

____

Which country did this flower originate?

____

List the different colors of this flower:

____

____

____

List the sources you used to research this flower:

Books: ____

____

Websites: ____

____

Other sources: ____

____

CREATIVE ARTS

Fill in the missing parts. Write the name of each flower from this section:

CREATIVE ARTS

Draw your favorite flower from this section. Use your imagination to draw the flower in its natural habitat. Add a house, forest, or animals!

KANSAS

The state flower is:
Sunflower

Find the botanical name: ____________________

How did this flower get its name? ______________________________

____

Is this flower an annual or perennial? __________________

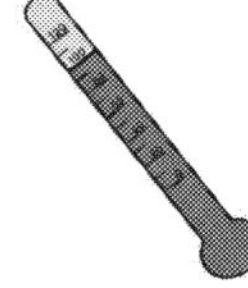

What range in temperature is best for this flower?
High: ___________ Low: ____________

How many hours of daily sunlight are needed for this flower? ______

Does this flower grow best in high or low altitude? ____________

List the type(s) of soil needed to grow the state flower: _________

____

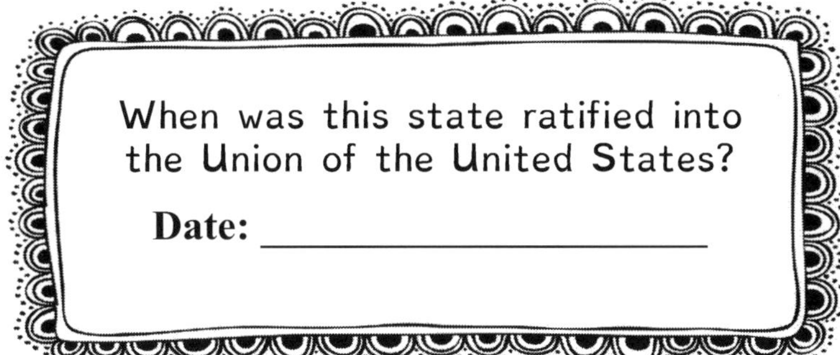

CREATIVE WRITING

In the space below, write a poem, short story, or a unique history tid-bit about the state flower. If this flower is in your state, and in bloom, try taping one to this page and press it in the book!

____

____

____

____

____

____

____

Which country did this flower originate?

____

List the different colors of this flower:

____

____

____

List the sources you used to research this flower:

Books: ____

____

Websites: ____

____

Other sources: ____

____

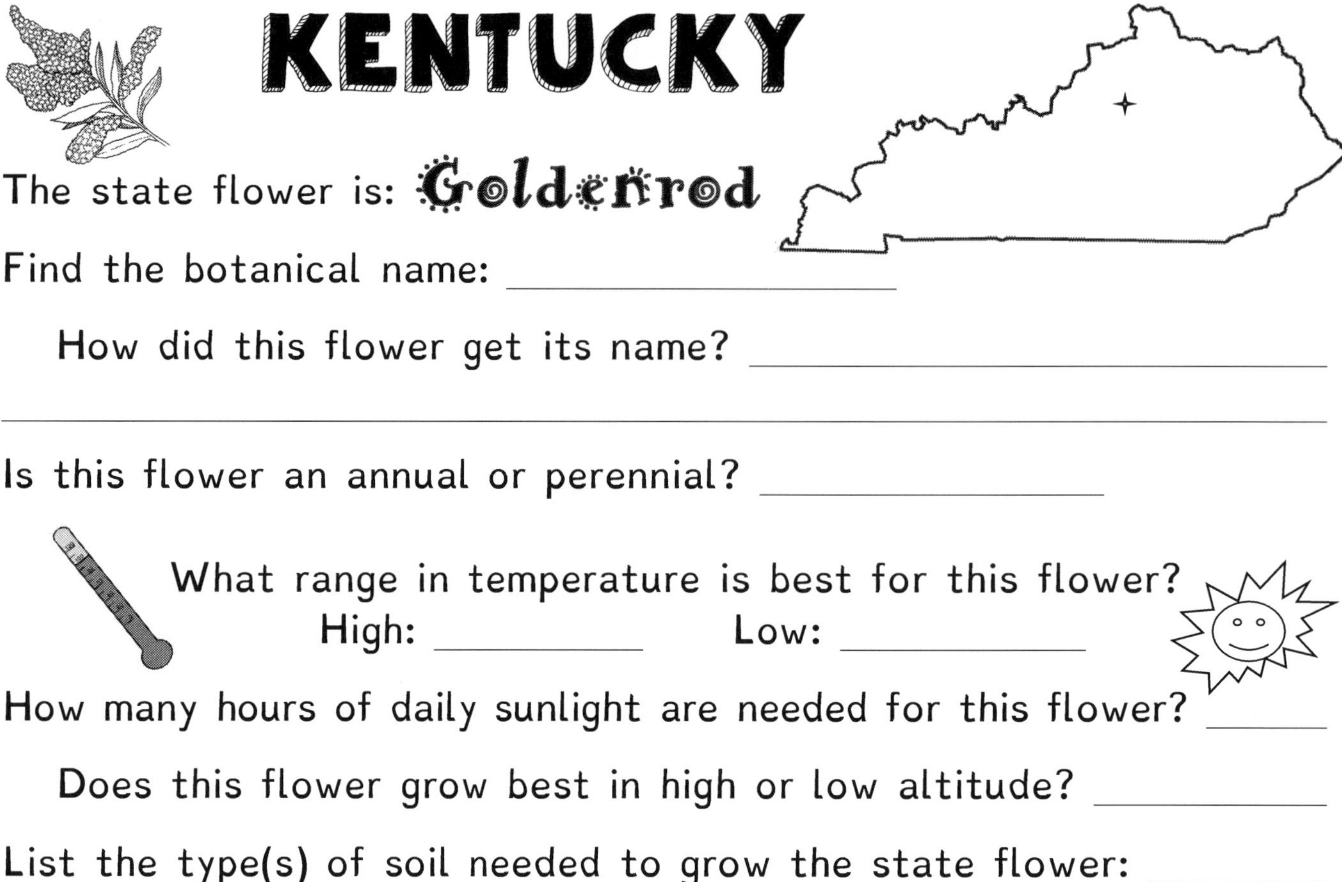

KENTUCKY

The state flower is: Goldenrod

Find the botanical name: ________________

How did this flower get its name? ________________________

____

Is this flower an annual or perennial? ______________

What range in temperature is best for this flower?

High: _________ Low: __________

How many hours of daily sunlight are needed for this flower? _____

Does this flower grow best in high or low altitude? _________

List the type(s) of soil needed to grow the state flower: _______

____

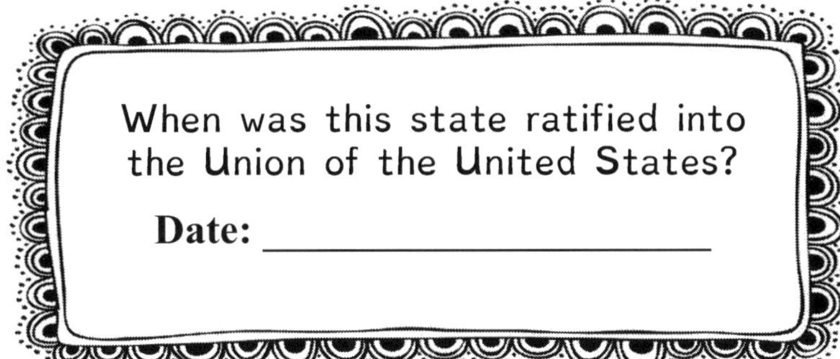

CREATIVE WRITING

In the space below, write a poem, short story, or a unique history tid-bit about the state flower. If this flower is in your state, and in bloom, try taping one to this page and press it in the book!

____

____

____

____

____

____

____

Which country did this flower originate?

____

List the different colors of this flower:

____

____

____

List the sources you used to research this flower:

Books: ____

____

Websites: ____

____

Other sources: ____

____

LOUISIANA

The state flower is: **Magnolia**

Find the botanical name: ____________________

How did this flower get its name? ______________________________

____

Is this flower an annual or perennial? __________________

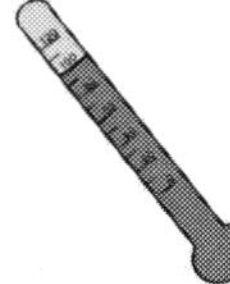

What range in temperature is best for this flower?

High: ___________ Low: _____________

How many hours of daily sunlight are needed for this flower? _______

Does this flower grow best in high or low altitude? __________

List the type(s) of soil needed to grow the state flower: ________

____

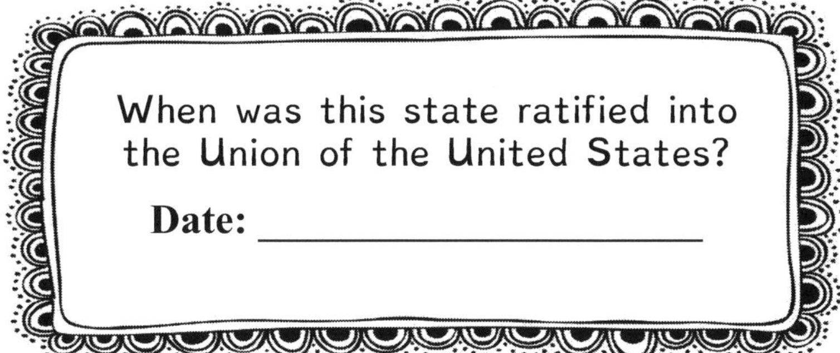

CREATIVE WRITING

In the space below, write a poem, short story, or a unique history tid-bit about the state flower. If this flower is in your state, and in bloom, try taping one to this page and press it in the book!

____

____

____

____

____

____

____

Which country did this flower originate?

____

List the different colors of this flower:

____

____

____

List the sources you used to research this flower:

Books: ____

____

Websites: ____

____

Other sources: ____

____

MAINE

The state flower is:

White Pine Cone & Tassel

Find the botanical name: ____________________

How did this flower get its name? ________________

____

Is this flower an annual or perennial? __________________

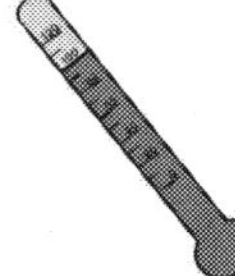

What range in temperature is best for this flower?
High: ___________ Low: _____________

How many hours of daily sunlight are needed for this flower? _____

Does this flower grow best in high or low altitude? _________

List the type(s) of soil needed to grow the state flower: _________

____

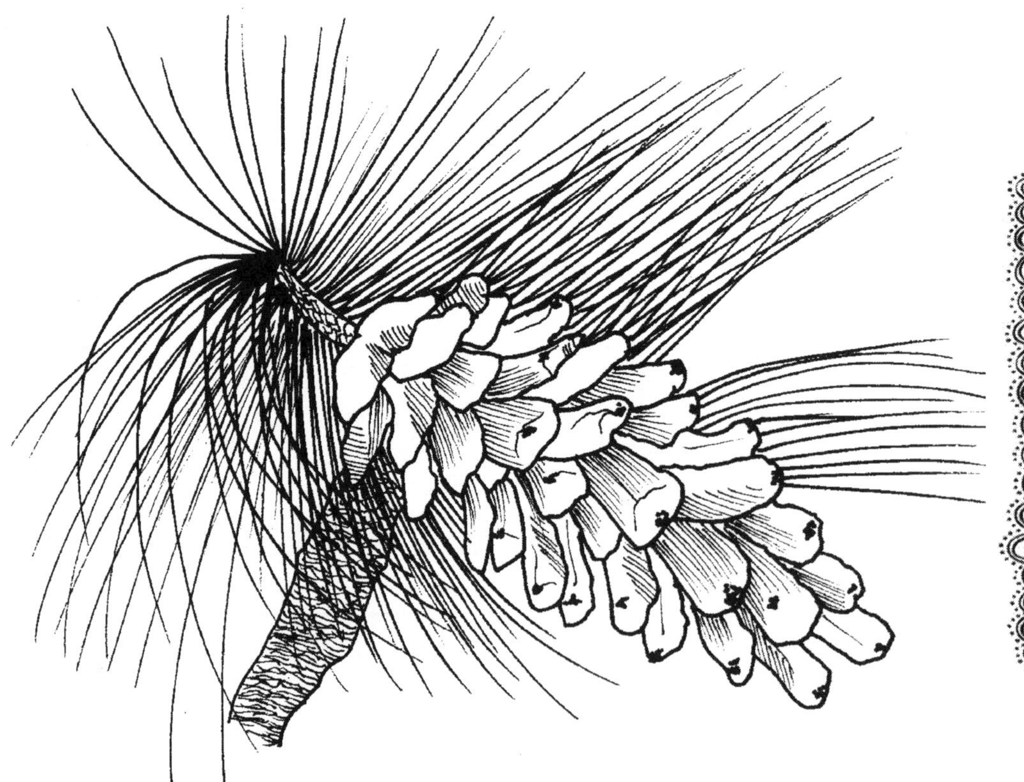

Interesting fact: Botanically, the white pine cone and tassel is not considered a flower, it is a gymnosperm, a tree that produces seeds without flowers.

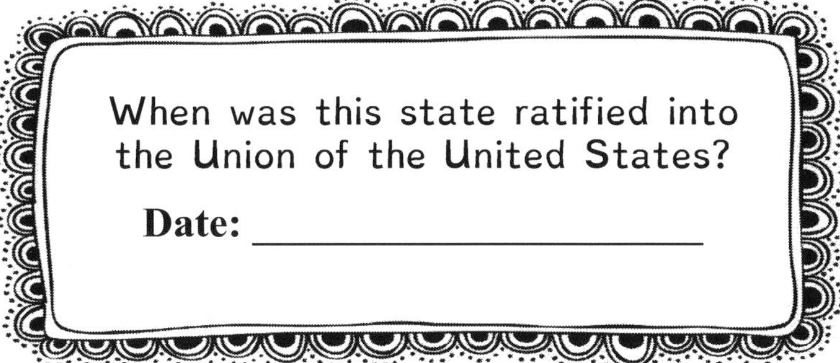

CREATIVE WRITING

In the space below, write a poem, short story, or a unique history tid-bit about the state flower. If this flower is in your state, and in bloom, try taping one to this page and press it in the book!

____

____

____

____

____

____

____

Which country did this flower originate?

____

List the different colors of this flower:

____

____

____

List the sources you used to research this flower:

Books: ____

____

Websites: ____

____

Other sources: ____

____

MARYLAND

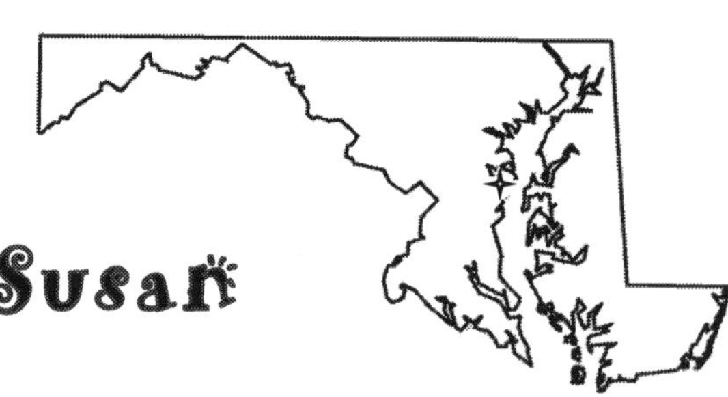

The state flower is: Black-eyed Susan

Find the botanical name: ____________________

How did this flower get its name? ______________________________

____

Is this flower an annual or perennial? __________________

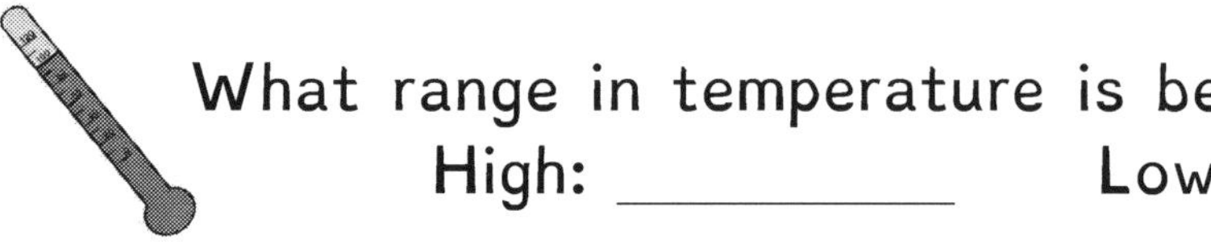

What range in temperature is best for this flower?

High: ___________ Low: _____________

How many hours of daily sunlight are needed for this flower? ______

Does this flower grow best in high or low altitude? ____________

List the type(s) of soil needed to grow the state flower: _________

_______________________________________ _____________________

____

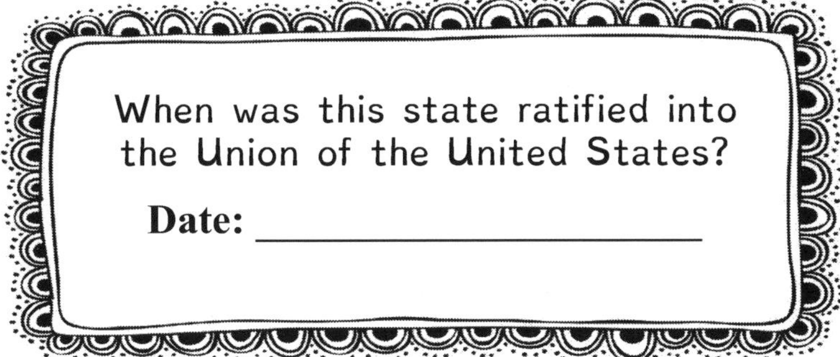

CREATIVE WRITING

In the space below, write a poem, short story, or a unique history tid-bit about the state flower. If this flower is in your state, and in bloom, try taping one to this page and press it in the book!

____

____

____

____

____

____

____

Which country did this flower originate?

____

List the different colors of this flower:

____

____

____

List the sources you used to research this flower:

Books: ____

____

Websites: ____

____

Other sources: ____

____

CREATIVE ARTS

Fill in the missing parts. Write the name of each flower from this section:

CREATIVE ARTS

Draw your favorite flower from this section. Use your imagination to draw the flower in its natural habitat. Add a house, forest, or animals!

MASSACHUSETTS

The state flower is: **Mayflower**

Find the botanical name: ____________________

How did this flower get its name? ______________________

____

Is this flower an annual or perennial? __________________

What range in temperature is best for this flower?
High: ___________ Low: _____________

How many hours of daily sunlight are needed for this flower? ______

Does this flower grow best in high or low altitude? ___________

List the type(s) of soil needed to grow the state flower: _________

____

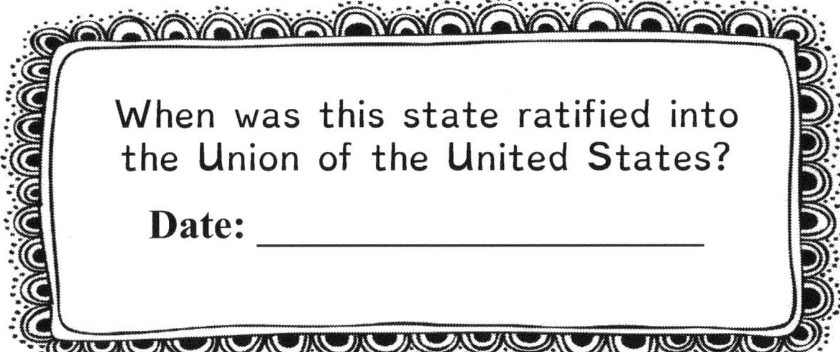

CREATIVE WRITING

In the space below, write a poem, short story, or a unique history tid-bit about the state flower. If this flower is in your state, and in bloom, try taping one to this page and press it in the book!

____

____

____

____

____

____

____

Which country did this flower originate?

____

List the different colors of this flower:

____

____

____

List the sources you used to research this flower:

Books: ____

____

Websites: ____

____

Other sources: ____

____

MICHIGAN

The state flower is: Apple Blossom

Find the botanical name: ______________________

How did this flower get its name? ______________________

____

Is this flower an annual or perennial? ____________________

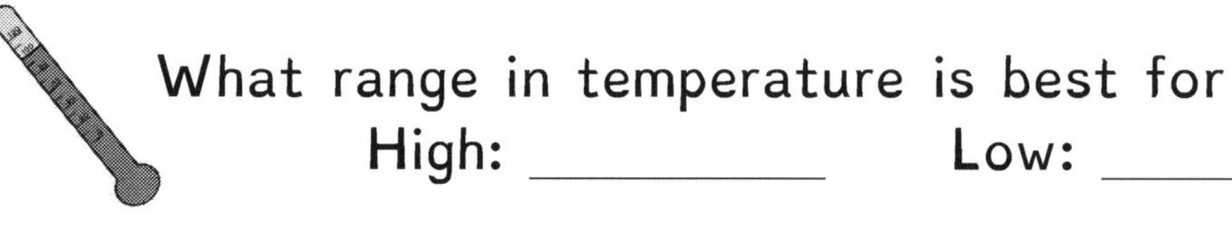

What range in temperature is best for this flower?

High: __________ Low: ____________

How many hours of daily sunlight are needed for this flower? ______

Does this flower grow best in high or low altitude? __________

List the type(s) of soil needed to grow the state flower: ________

____

Which other state declared Apple Blossom as their state flower?

____

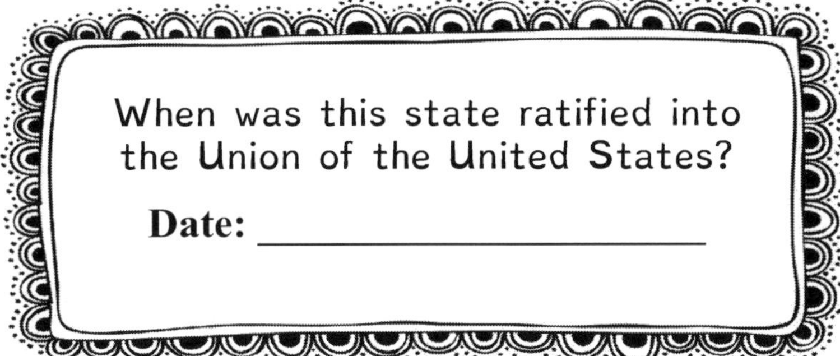

CREATIVE WRITING

In the space below, write a poem, short story, or a unique history tid-bit about the state flower. If this flower is in your state, and in bloom, try taping one to this page and press it in the book!

____

____

____

____

____

____

____

Which country did this flower originate?

____

List the different colors of this flower:

____

____

____

List the sources you used to research this flower:

Books: ____

____

Websites: ____

____

Other sources: ____

____

MINNESOTA

The state flower is:

Pink and White Lady's Slipper

Find the botanical name: ____________________

How did this flower get its name? ______________________________

____

Is this flower an annual or perennial? __________________

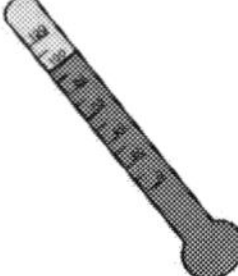

What range in temperature is best for this flower?
High: ___________ Low: _____________

How many hours of daily sunlight are needed for this flower? _______

Does this flower grow best in high or low altitude? ____________

List the type(s) of soil needed to grow the state flower: _________

____

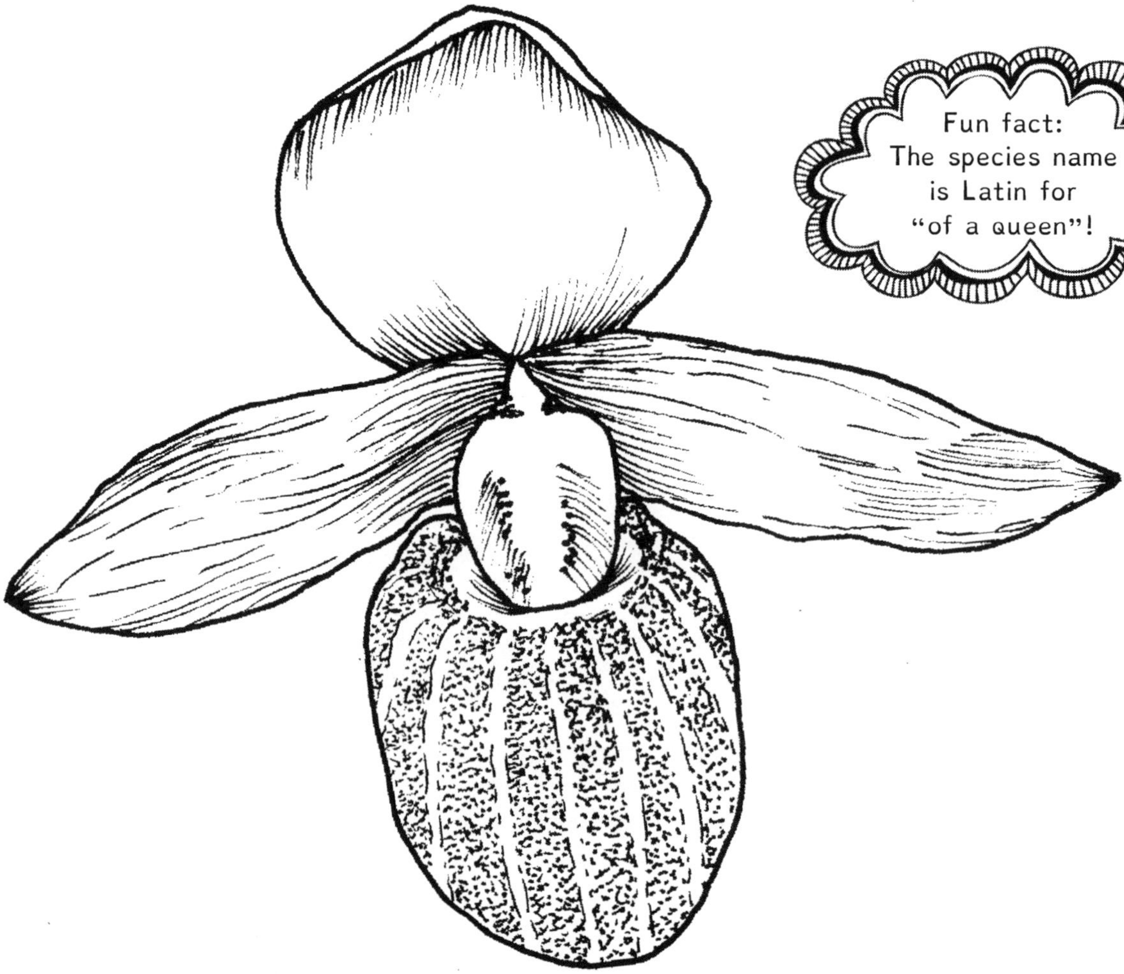

Fun fact:
The species name
is Latin for
"of a queen"!

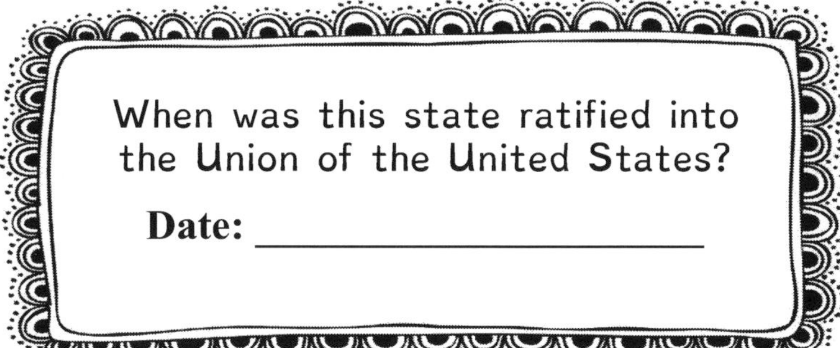

CREATIVE WRITING

In the space below, write a poem, short story, or a unique history tid-bit about the state flower. If this flower is in your state, and in bloom, try taping one to this page and press it in the book!

____

____

____

____

____

____

____

Which country did this flower originate?

____

List the different colors of this flower:

____

____

____

List the sources you used to research this flower:

Books: ____

____

Websites: ____

____

Other sources: ____________________________________

____

MISSISSIPPI

The state flower is: **Magnolia**

Find the botanical name: ____________________

How did this flower get its name? ______________________________

____

Is this flower an annual or perennial? __________________

What range in temperature is best for this flower?
High: ___________ Low: _____________

How many hours of daily sunlight are needed for this flower? ______

Does this flower grow best in high or low altitude? ____________

List the type(s) of soil needed to grow the state flower: _________

____

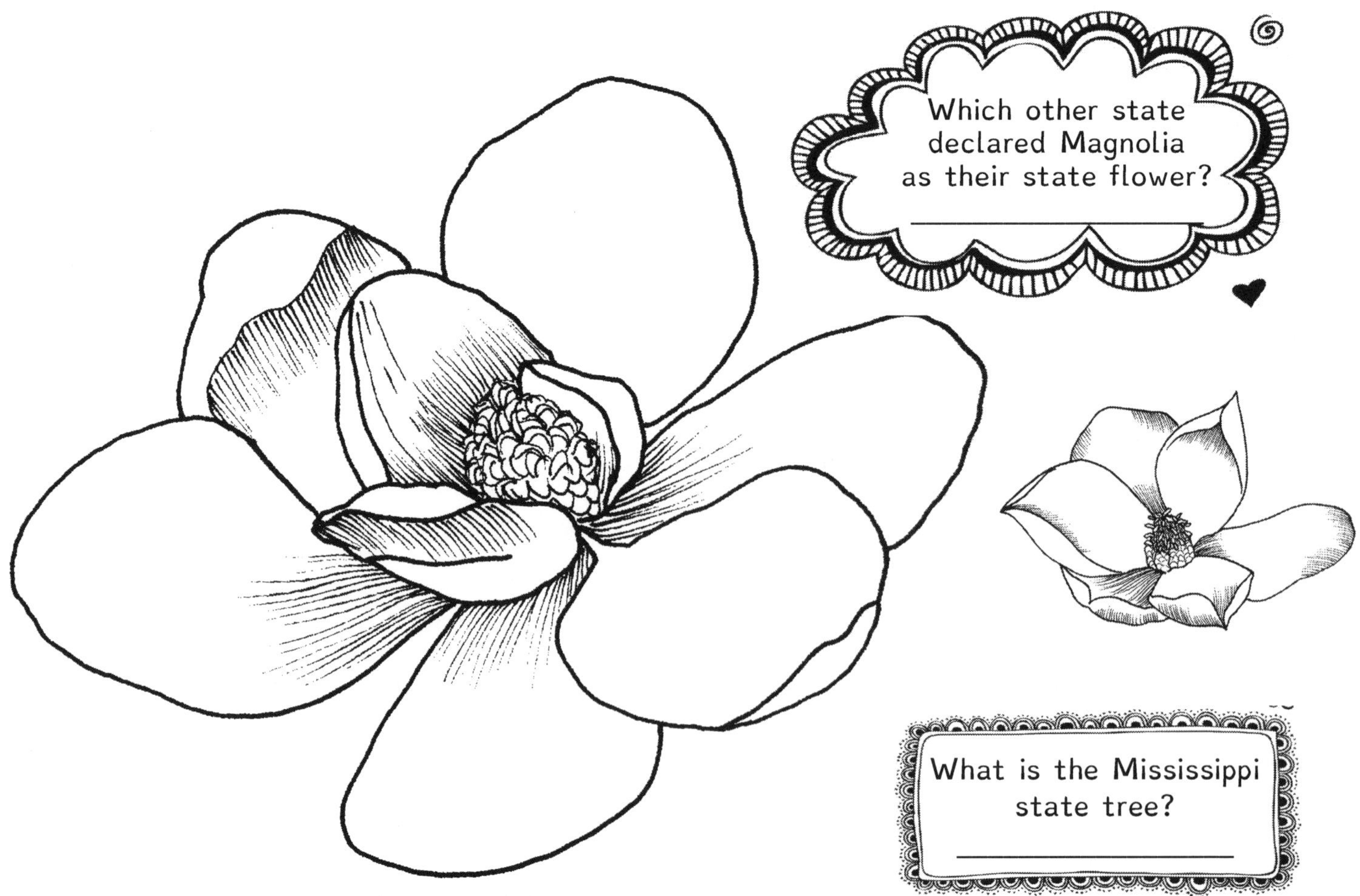

Which other state declared Magnolia as their state flower?

____

What is the Mississippi state tree?

____

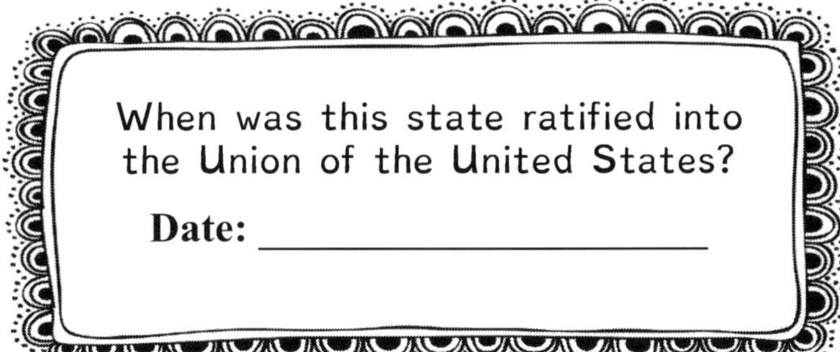

CREATIVE WRITING

In the space below, write a poem, short story, or a unique history tid-bit about the state flower. If this flower is in your state, and in bloom, try taping one to this page and press it in the book!

____

____

____

____

____

____

____

Which country did this flower originate?

____

List the different colors of this flower:

____

____

____

List the sources you used to research this flower:

Books: ____

____

Websites: ____

____

Other sources: ____

____

MISSOURI

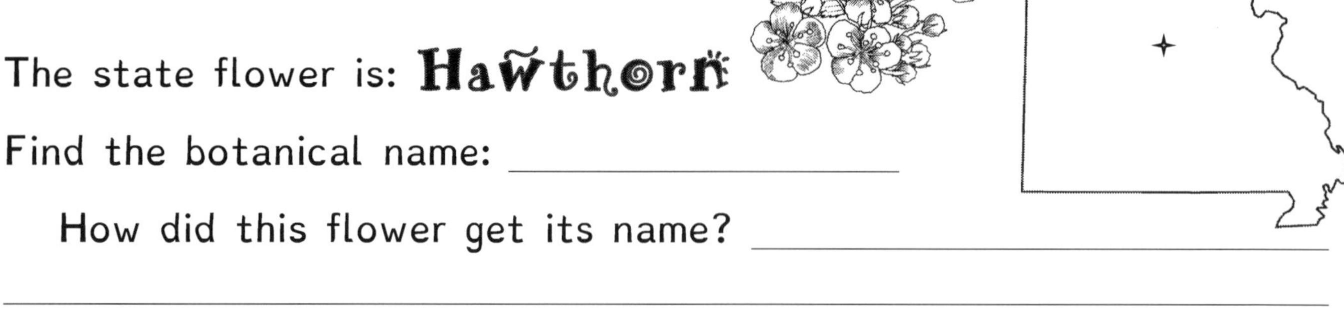

The state flower is: **Hawthorn**

Find the botanical name: ____________________

How did this flower get its name? ______________________________

____

Is this flower an annual or perennial? __________________

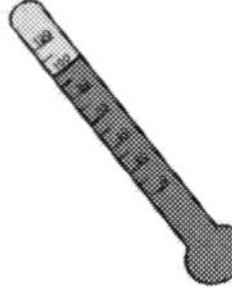

What range in temperature is best for this flower?
High: ___________ Low: _____________

How many hours of daily sunlight are needed for this flower? ______

Does this flower grow best in high or low altitude? ____________

List the type(s) of soil needed to grow the state flower: _________

____

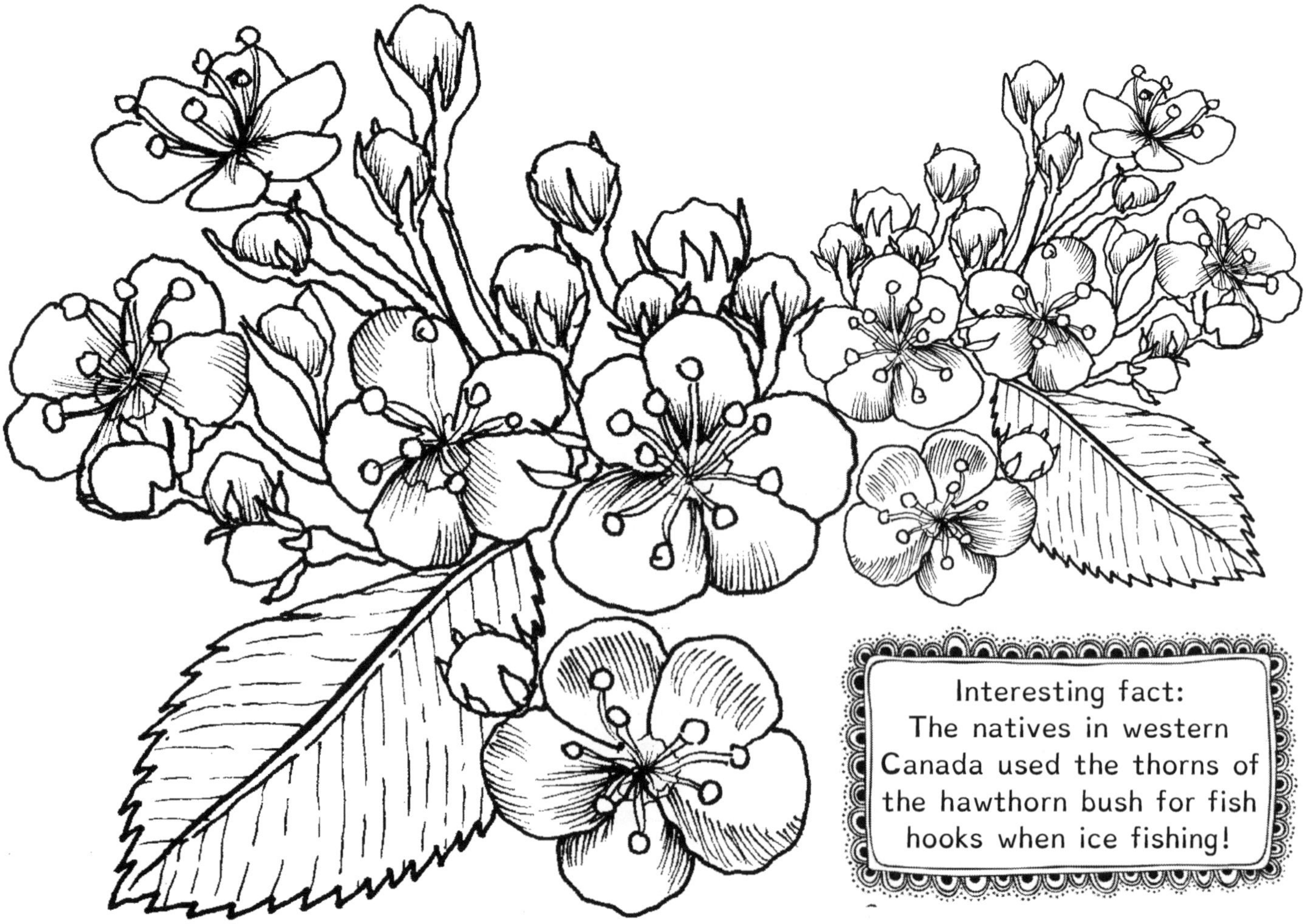

Interesting fact:
The natives in western Canada used the thorns of the hawthorn bush for fish hooks when ice fishing!

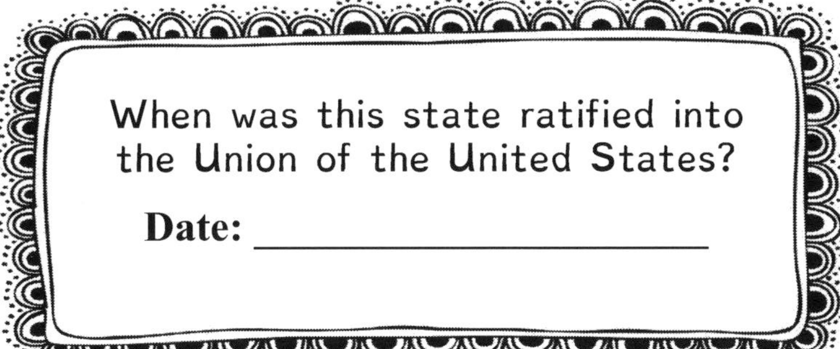

CREATIVE WRITING

In the space below, write a poem, short story, or a unique history tid-bit about the state flower. If this flower is in your state, and in bloom, try taping one to this page and press it in the book!

____

____

____

____

____

____

____

Which country did this flower originate?

____

List the different colors of this flower:

____

____

____

List the sources you used to research this flower:

Books: ____

____

Websites: ____

____

Other sources: ____

____

CREATIVE ARTS

Fill in the missing parts. Write the name of each flower from this section:

CREATIVE ARTS

Draw your favorite flower from this section. Use your imagination to draw the flower in its natural habitat. Add a house, forest, or animals!

MONTANA

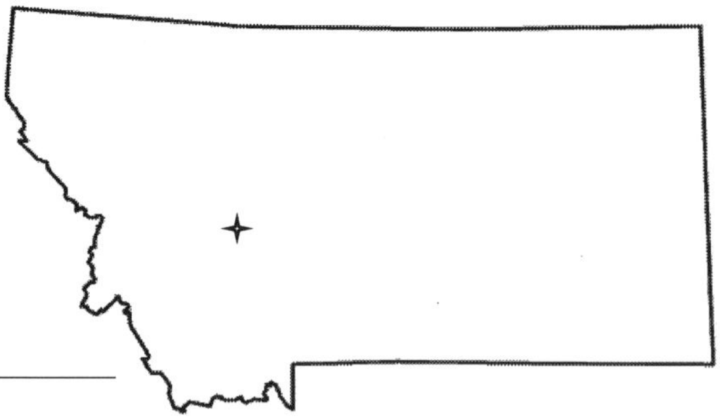

The state flower is: Bitterroot

Find the botanical name: ____________________

How did this flower get its name? ______________________________

____

Is this flower an annual or perennial? __________________

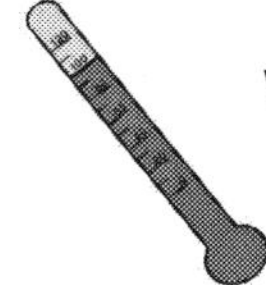

What range in temperature is best for this flower?

High: ___________ Low: _____________

How many hours of daily sunlight are needed for this flower? ______

Does this flower grow best in high or low altitude? ___________

List the type(s) of soil needed to grow the state flower: _________

____

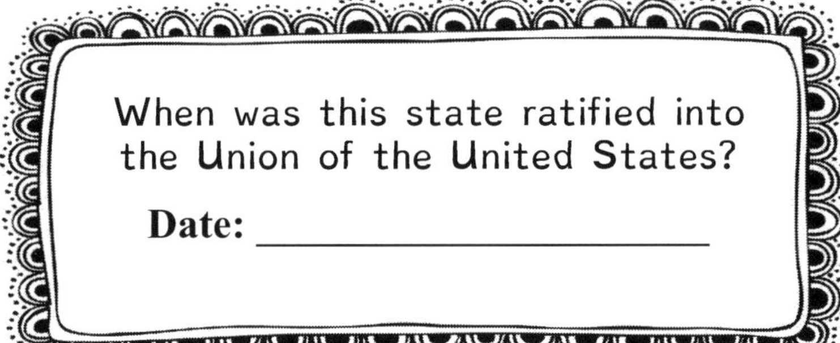

CREATIVE WRITING

In the space below, write a poem, short story, or a unique history tid-bit about the state flower. If this flower is in your state, and in bloom, try taping one to this page and press it in the book!

____

____

____

____

____

____

____

Which country did this flower originate?

____

List the different colors of this flower:

____

____

____

List the sources you used to research this flower:

Books: ____

____

Websites: ____

____

Other sources: ____

____

NEBRASKA

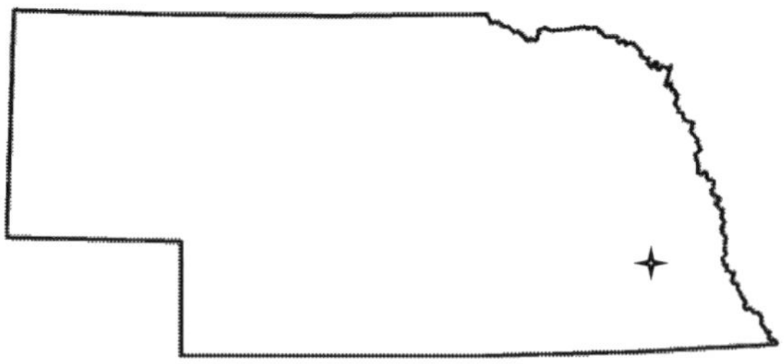

The state flower is: **Goldenrod**

Find the botanical name: ____________________

How did this flower get its name? ______________________________

____

Is this flower an annual or perennial? __________________

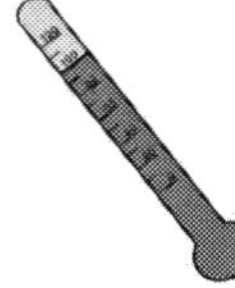

What range in temperature is best for this flower?
High: ___________ Low: _____________

How many hours of daily sunlight are needed for this flower? ______

Does this flower grow best in high or low altitude? ____________

List the type(s) of soil needed to grow the state flower: _________

____

Which other state declared Goldenrod as their state flower?

____

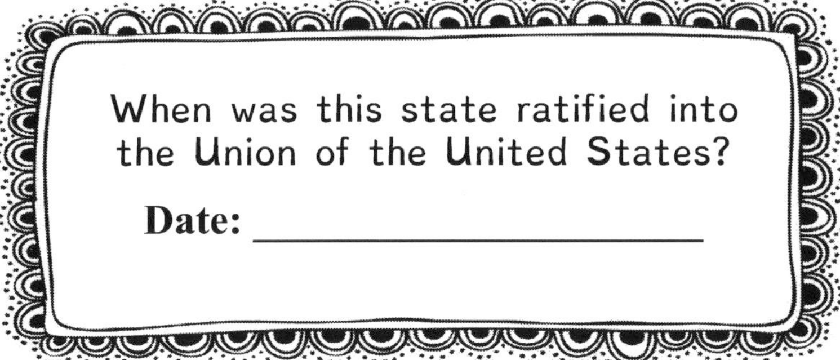

CREATIVE WRITING

In the space below, write a poem, short story, or a unique history tid-bit about the state flower. If this flower is in your state, and in bloom, try taping one to this page and press it in the book!

____

____

____

____

____

____

____

Which country did this flower originate?

____

List the different colors of this flower:

____

____

____

List the sources you used to research this flower:

Books: ______________________________________

____

Websites: ___________________________________

____

Other sources: _______________________________

____

NEVADA

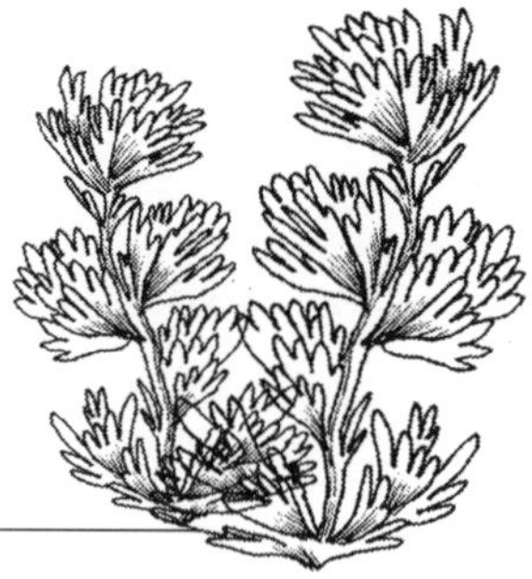

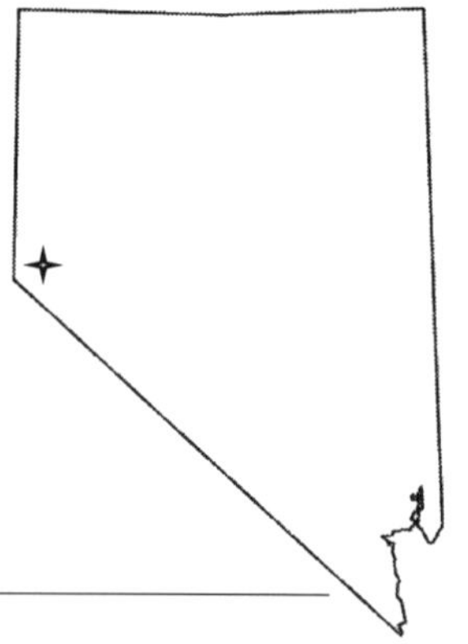

The state flower is: **Sagebrush**

Find the botanical name: ____________________

How did this flower get its name? ____________________

____

Is this flower an annual or perennial? ______________

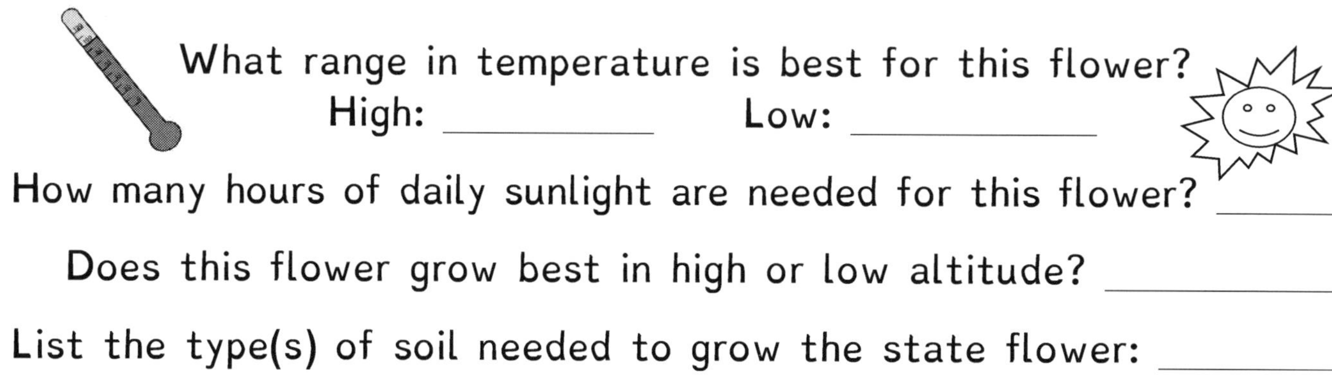

What range in temperature is best for this flower?

High: __________ Low: __________

How many hours of daily sunlight are needed for this flower? ______

Does this flower grow best in high or low altitude? ________

List the type(s) of soil needed to grow the state flower: ________

____

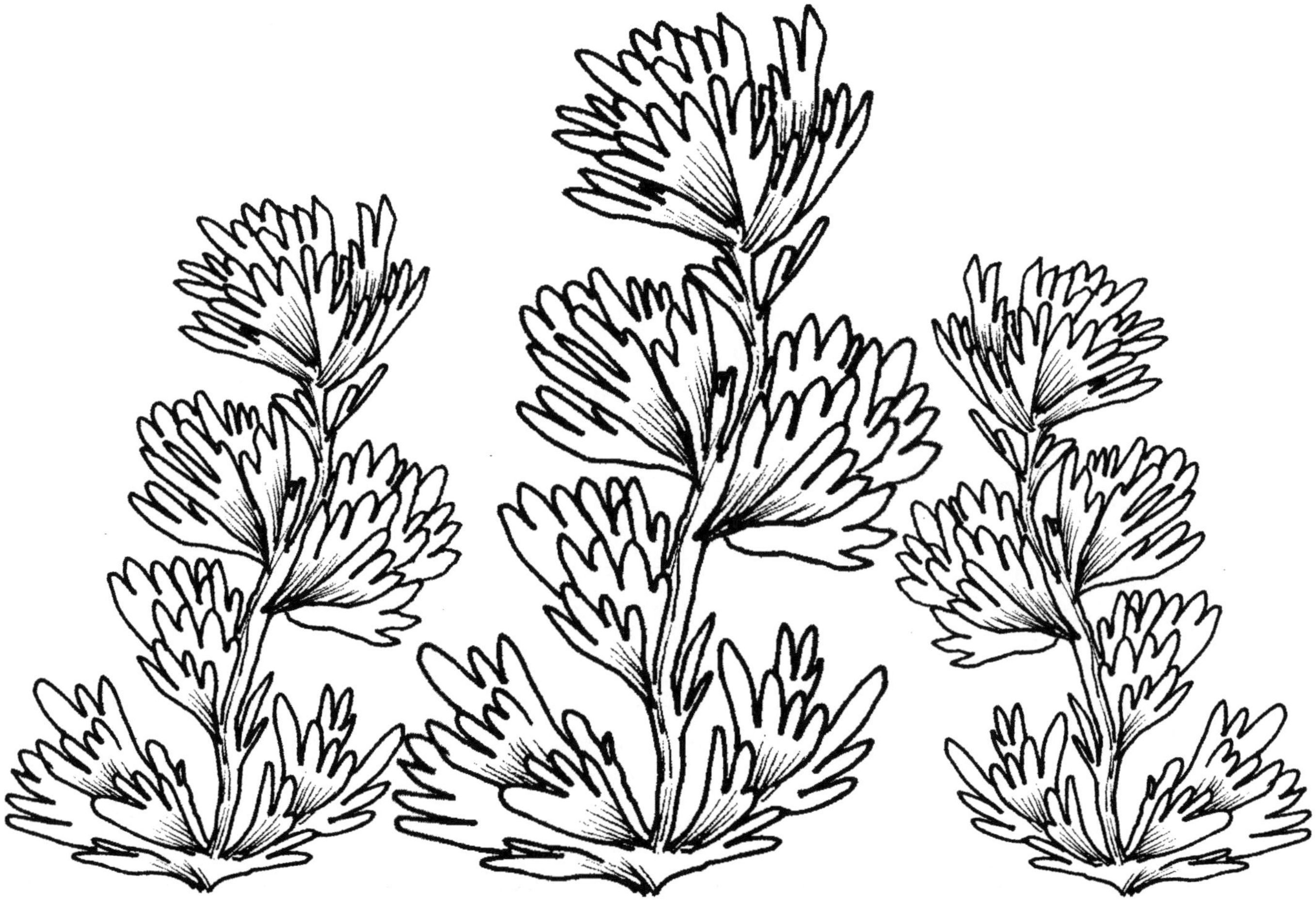

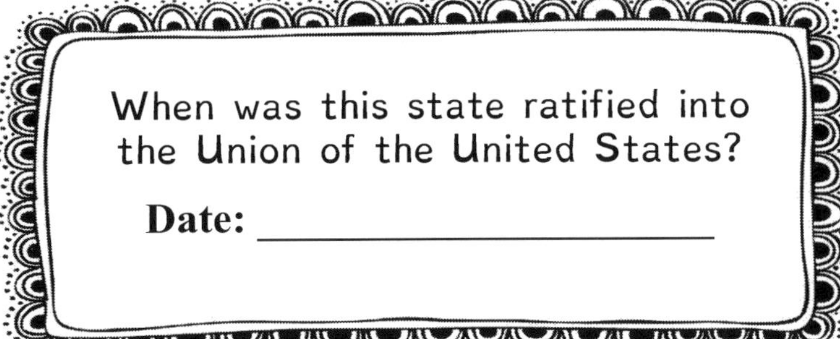

CREATIVE WRITING

In the space below, write a poem, short story, or a unique history tid-bit about the state flower. If this flower is in your state, and in bloom, try taping one to this page and press it in the book!

____

____

____

____

____

____

____

Which country did this flower originate?

____

List the different colors of this flower:

____

____

____

List the sources you used to research this flower:

Books: ____

____

Websites: ____

____

Other sources: ____

____

NEW HAMPSHIRE

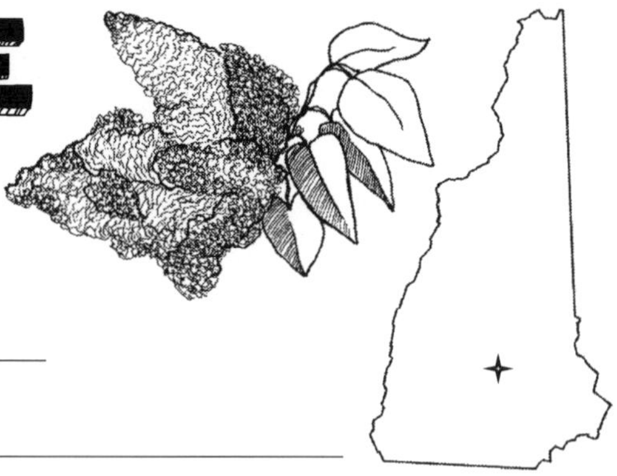

The state flower is: **Purple Lilac**

Find the botanical name: ____________________

How did this flower get its name? ____________________

____

Is this flower an annual or perennial? __________________

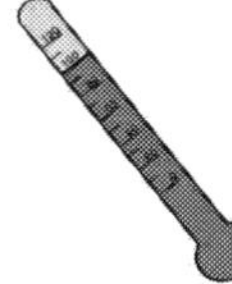

What range in temperature is best for this flower?
High: __________ Low: ____________

How many hours of daily sunlight are needed for this flower? ______

Does this flower grow best in high or low altitude? ___________

List the type(s) of soil needed to grow the state flower: ________

____

Fun fact:
Our ancestors placed a bouquet of lilacs next to their bed to give them a good night's sleep!

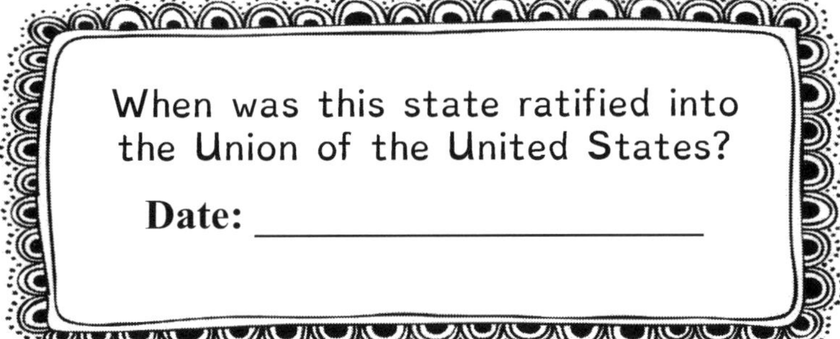

CREATIVE WRITING

In the space below, write a poem, short story, or a unique history tid-bit about the state flower. If this flower is in your state, and in bloom, try taping one to this page and press it in the book!

____

____

____

____

____

____

____

Which country did this flower originate?

____

List the different colors of this flower:

____

____

____

List the sources you used to research this flower:

Books: ______________________________________

____

Websites: ___________________________________

____

Other sources: _______________________________

____

NEW JERSEY

The state flower is: **Violet**

Find the botanical name: ________________

How did this flower get its name? ________________

____

Is this flower an annual or perennial? ______________

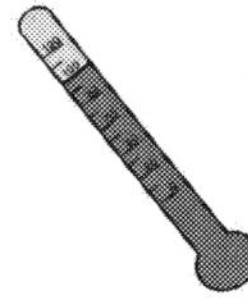

What range in temperature is best for this flower?

High: ________ Low: __________

How many hours of daily sunlight are needed for this flower? _____

Does this flower grow best in high or low altitude? __________

List the type(s) of soil needed to grow the state flower: _______

____

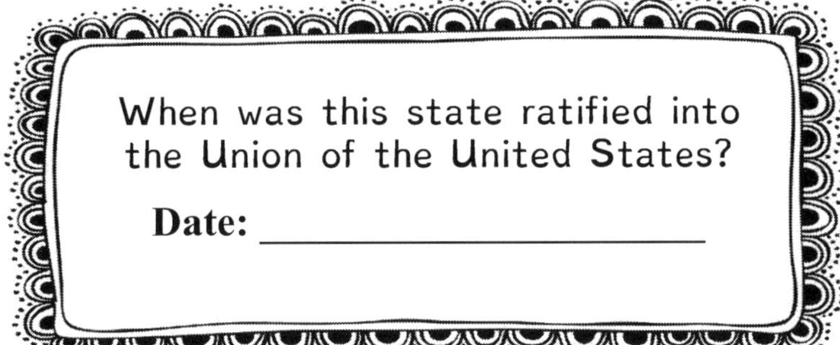

CREATIVE WRITING

In the space below, write a poem, short story, or a unique history tid-bit about the state flower. If this flower is in your state, and in bloom, try taping one to this page and press it in the book!

____

____

____

____

____

____

____

Which country did this flower originate?

____

List the different colors of this flower:

____

____

____

List the sources you used to research this flower:

Books: ____

____

Websites: ____

____

Other sources: ____

____

CREATIVE ARTS

Fill in the missing parts. Write the name of each flower from this section:

CREATIVE ARTS

Draw your favorite flower from this section. Use your imagination to draw the flower in its natural habitat. Add a house, forest, or animals!

NEW MEXICO

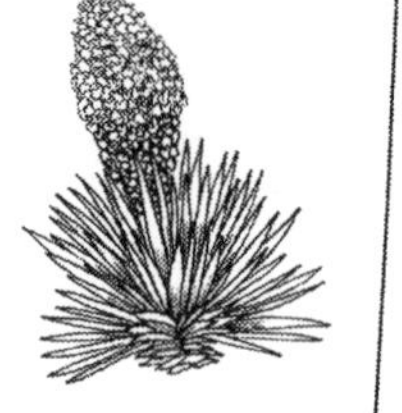

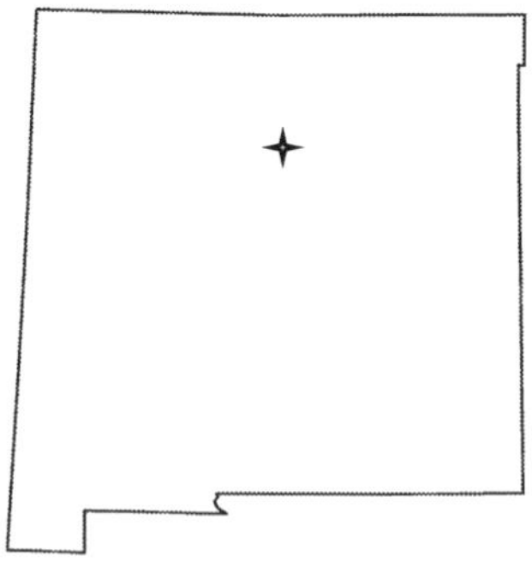

The state flower is: **Yucca Flower**

Find the botanical name: ____________________

How did this flower get its name? ______________________________

____

Is this flower an annual or perennial? __________________

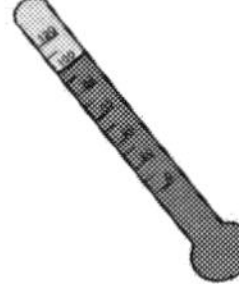

What range in temperature is best for this flower?

High: ___________ Low: _____________

How many hours of daily sunlight are needed for this flower? ______

Does this flower grow best in high or low altitude? ____________

List the type(s) of soil needed to grow the state flower: _________

____

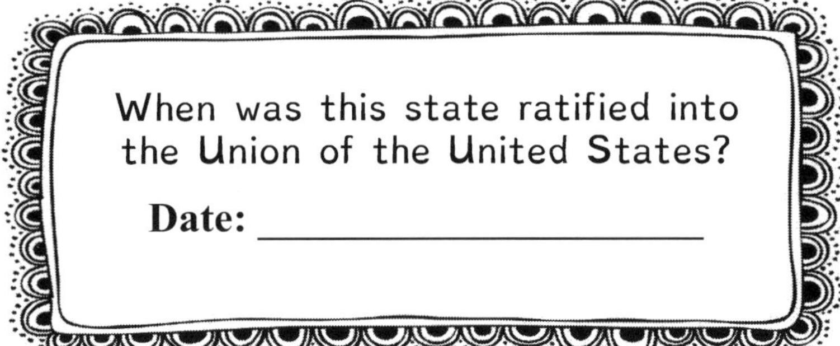

CREATIVE WRITING

In the space below, write a poem, short story, or a unique history tid-bit about the state flower. If this flower is in your state, and in bloom, try taping one to this page and press it in the book!

____

____

____

____

____

____

____

Which country did this flower originate?

____

List the different colors of this flower:

____

____

____

List the sources you used to research this flower:

Books: ______________________________________

____

Websites: ___________________________________

____

Other sources: ______________________________

____

NEW YORK

The state flower is: **Rose**

Find the botanical name: ____________________

How did this flower get its name? ______________________

____

Is this flower an annual or perennial? __________________

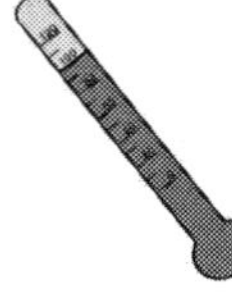

What range in temperature is best for this flower?

High: ___________ Low: _____________

How many hours of daily sunlight are needed for this flower? ______

Does this flower grow best in high or low altitude? ____________

List the type(s) of soil needed to grow the state flower: _________

____

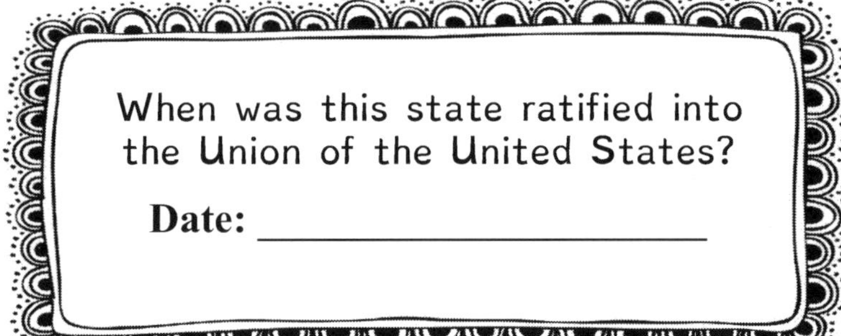

CREATIVE WRITING

In the space below, write a poem, short story, or a unique history tid-bit about the state flower. If this flower is in your state, and in bloom, try taping one to this page and press it in the book!

____

____

____

____

____

____

____

Which country did this flower originate?

____

List the different colors of this flower:

____

____

____

List the sources you used to research this flower:

Books: ____

____

Websites: ____

____

Other sources: ____

____

NORTH CAROLINA

The state flower is:

Flowering Dogwood

Find the botanical name: ____________________

How did this flower get its name? ______________________________

____

Is this flower an annual or perennial? __________________

What range in temperature is best for this flower?

High: ___________ Low: _____________

How many hours of daily sunlight are needed for this flower? ______

Does this flower grow best in high or low altitude? ______

List the type(s) of soil needed to grow the state flower: _________

____

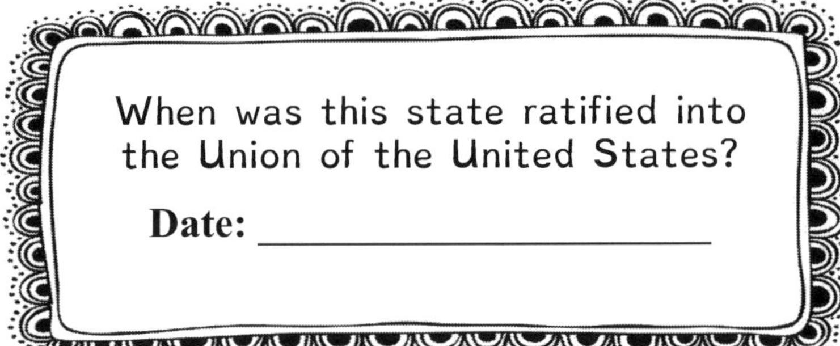

CREATIVE WRITING

In the space below, write a poem, short story, or a unique history tid-bit about the state flower. If this flower is in your state, and in bloom, try taping one to this page and press it in the book!

____

____

____

____

____

____

____

Which country did this flower originate?

____

List the different colors of this flower:

____

____

____

List the sources you used to research this flower:

Books: ____

____

Websites: ____

____

Other sources: ____

____

NORTH DAKOTA

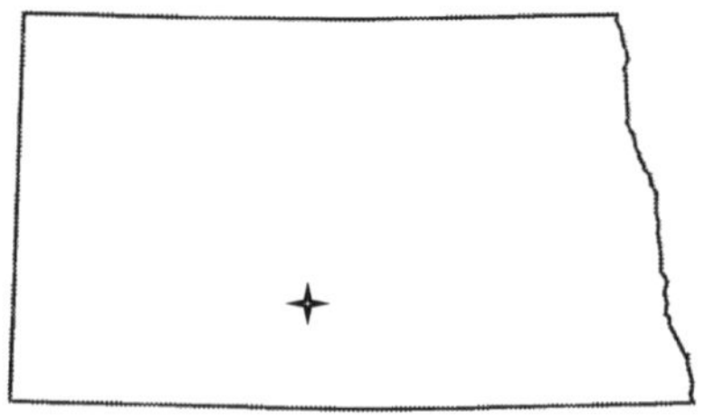

The state flower is:

Wild Prairie Rose

Find the botanical name: ____________

How did this flower get its name? ____________

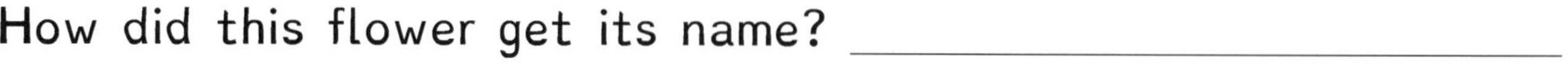

Is this flower an annual or perennial? ____________

What range in temperature is best for this flower?
High: ________ Low: ________

How many hours of daily sunlight are needed for this flower? ______

Does this flower grow best in high or low altitude? ______

List the type(s) of soil needed to grow the state flower: ______

Four states picked flowers in the Rose family for their state flower. Name the other three states:

____

____

____

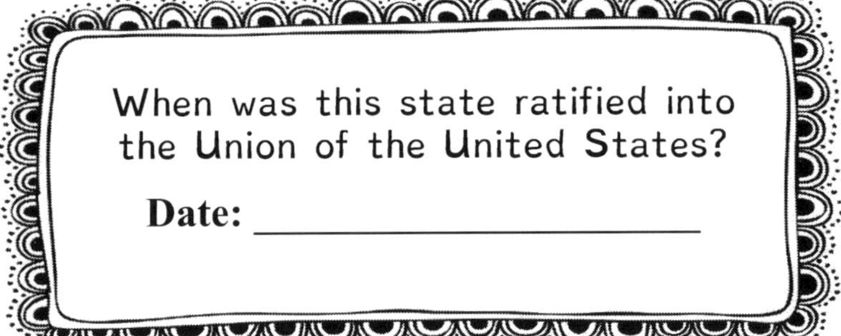

CREATIVE WRITING

In the space below, write a poem, short story, or a unique history tid-bit about the state flower. If this flower is in your state, and in bloom, try taping one to this page and press it in the book!

____

____

____

____

____

____

____

Which country did this flower originate?

____

List the different colors of this flower:

____

____

____

List the sources you used to research this flower:

Books: ____

____

Websites: ____

____

Other sources: ____

____

OHIO

The state flower is:

Scarlet Carnation

Find the botanical name: ____________________

How did this flower get its name? ____________________

____

Is this flower an annual or perennial? ____________________

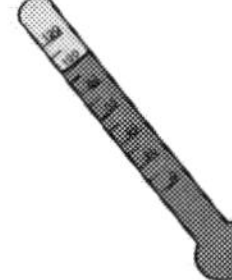

What range in temperature is best for this flower?
High: __________ Low: __________

How many hours of daily sunlight are needed for this flower? ______

Does this flower grow best in high or low altitude? ________

List the type(s) of soil needed to grow the state flower: ________

____

Interesting fact:
The original natural flower color is bright pinkish-purple, but around 1996 a company used genetic engineering to extract certain genes from petunia and snapdragon flowers to breed the different colors.

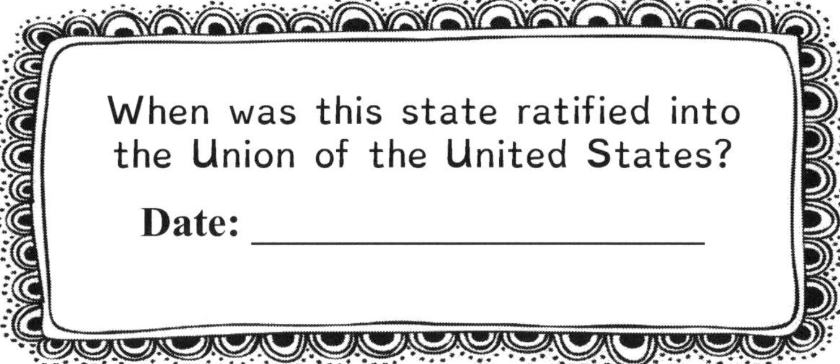

CREATIVE WRITING

In the space below, write a poem, short story, or a unique history tid-bit about the state flower. If this flower is in your state, and in bloom, try taping one to this page and press it in the book!

____

____

____

____

____

____

____

Which country did this flower originate?

____

List the different colors of this flower:

____

____

____

List the sources you used to research this flower:

Books: ____

____

Websites: ____

____

Other sources: ____

____

CREATIVE ARTS

Fill in the missing parts. Write the name of each flower from this section:

CREATIVE ARTS

Draw your favorite flower from this section. Use your imagination to draw the flower in its natural habitat. Add a house, forest, or animals!

OKLAHOMA

The state flower is: **Mistletoe**

Find the botanical name: ____________________

How did this flower get its name? ______________________________

____

Is this flower an annual or perennial? __________________

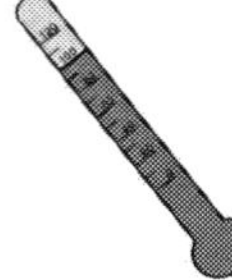

What range in temperature is best for this flower?
High: ___________ Low: ___________

How many hours of daily sunlight are needed for this flower? ______

Does this flower grow best in high or low altitude? ___________

List the type(s) of soil needed to grow the state flower: ________

____

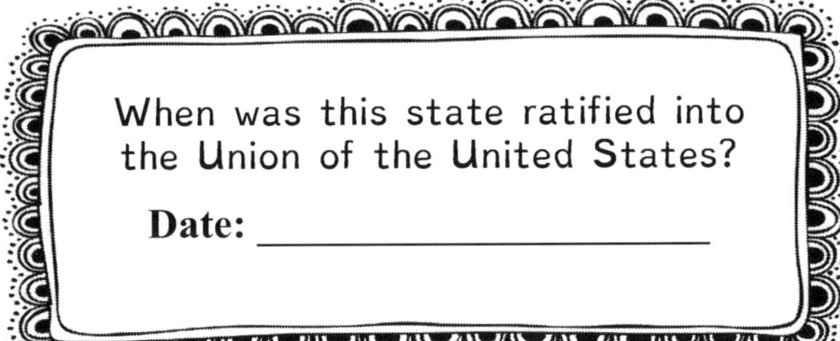

CREATIVE WRITING

In the space below, write a poem, short story, or a unique history tid-bit about the state flower. If this flower is in your state, and in bloom, try taping one to this page and press it in the book!

____

____

____

____

____

____

____

Which country did this flower originate?

____

List the different colors of this flower:

____

____

____

List the sources you used to research this flower:

Books: ____

____

Websites: ____

____

Other sources: ____

____

OREGON

The state flower is: **Oregon Grape**

Find the botanical name: ____________________

How did this flower get its name? ______________________________

____

Is this flower an annual or perennial? __________________

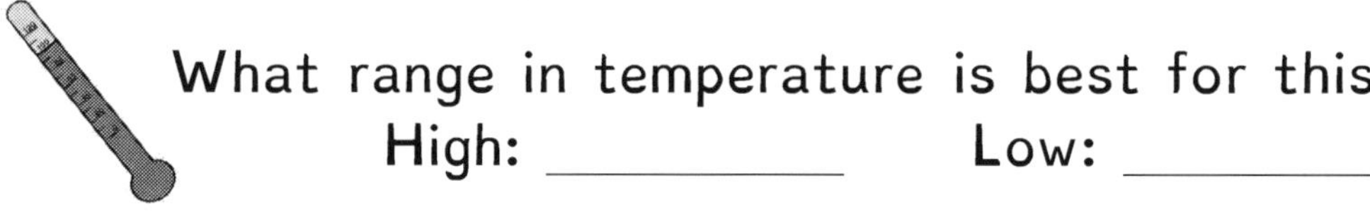

What range in temperature is best for this flower?

High: ___________ Low: _____________

How many hours of daily sunlight are needed for this flower? _______

Does this flower grow best in high or low altitude? ____________

List the type(s) of soil needed to grow the state flower: _________

____

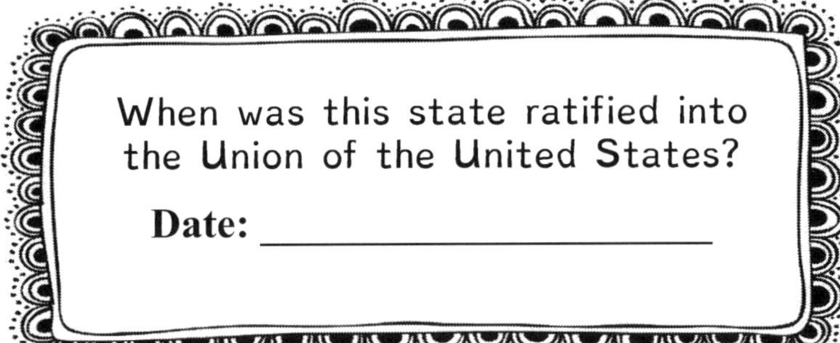

CREATIVE WRITING

In the space below, write a poem, short story, or a unique history tid-bit about the state flower. If this flower is in your state, and in bloom, try taping one to this page and press it in the book!

____

____

____

____

____

____

____

Which country did this flower originate?

____

List the different colors of this flower:

____

____

____

List the sources you used to research this flower:

Books: ____

____

Websites: ____

____

Other sources: ____

____

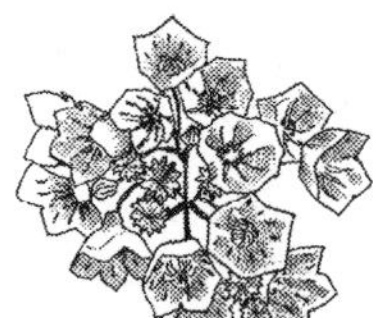

PENNSYLVANIA

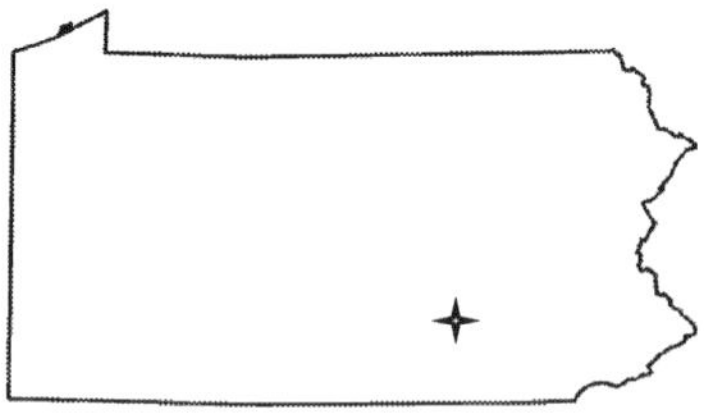

The state flower is: **Mountain Laurel**

Find the botanical name: ____________________

How did this flower get its name? ______________________________

____

Is this flower an annual or perennial? __________________

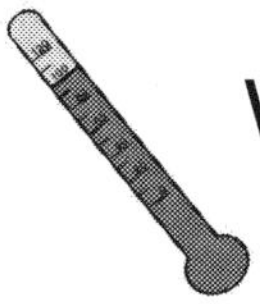

What range in temperature is best for this flower?

High: ___________ Low: _____________

How many hours of daily sunlight are needed for this flower? _______

Does this flower grow best in high or low altitude? ____________

List the type(s) of soil needed to grow the state flower: _________

____

Which other state declared Mountain Laurel as their state flower?

____

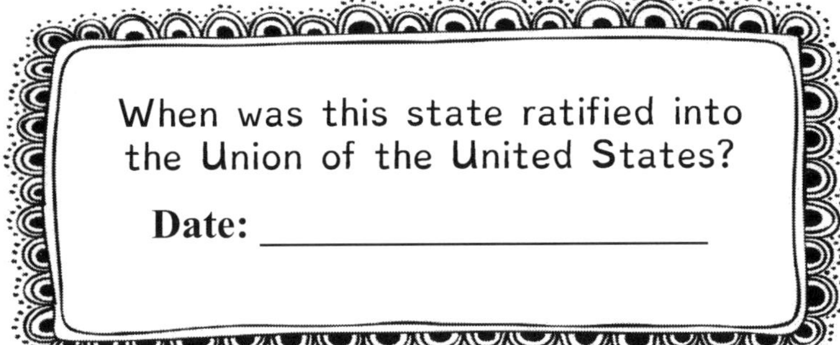

CREATIVE WRITING

In the space below, write a poem, short story, or a unique history tid-bit about the state flower. If this flower is in your state, and in bloom, try taping one to this page and press it in the book!

____

____

____

____

____

____

____

Which country did this flower originate?

____

List the different colors of this flower:

____

____

____

List the sources you used to research this flower:

Books: ____

____

Websites: ____

____

Other sources: ____

____

RHODE ISLAND

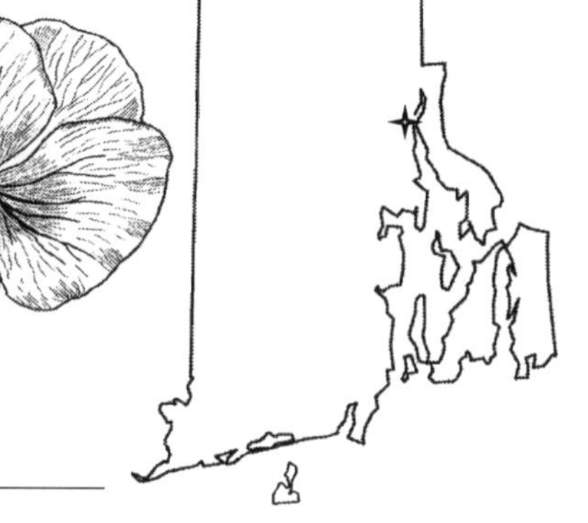

The state flower is: **Violet**

Find the botanical name: ______________

How did this flower get its name? ______________

____

Is this flower an annual or perennial? ______________

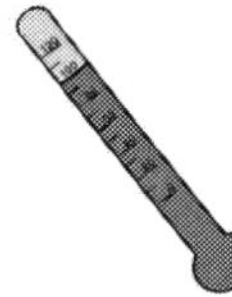

What range in temperature is best for this flower?
High: __________ Low: __________

How many hours of daily sunlight are needed for this flower? ______

Does this flower grow best in high or low altitude? __________

List the type(s) of soil needed to grow the state flower: ________

____

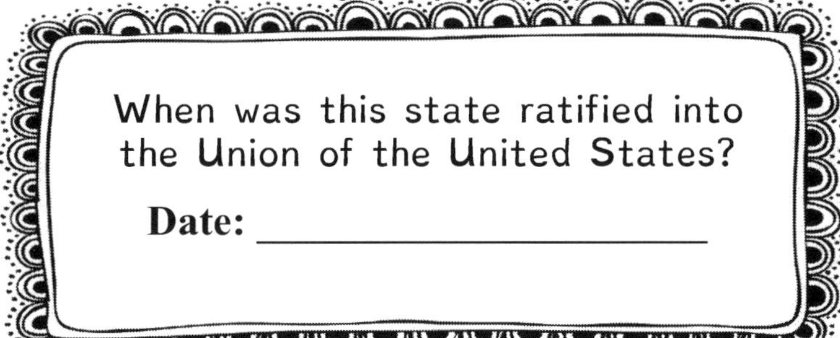

When was this state ratified into the Union of the United States?

Date: ______________________

Find this state on page 5 and use a different color to fill it in.

CREATIVE WRITING

In the space below, write a poem, short story, or a unique history tid-bit about the state flower. If this flower is in your state, and in bloom, try taping one to this page and press it in the book!

____

____

____

____

____

____

____

Which country did this flower originate?

____

List the different colors of this flower:

____

____

____

List the sources you used to research this flower:

Books: ____

____

Websites: ____

____

Other sources: ____

____

SOUTH CAROLINA

The state flower is: Yellow Jessamine

Find the botanical name: ____________________

How did this flower get its name? __________________

____

Is this flower an annual or perennial? __________________

What range in temperature is best for this flower?
High: ___________ Low: _____________

How many hours of daily sunlight are needed for this flower? ______

Does this flower grow best in high or low altitude? ____________

List the type(s) of soil needed to grow the state flower: _________

____

Interesting fact: The Yellow Jessamine can be lethal to cattle!

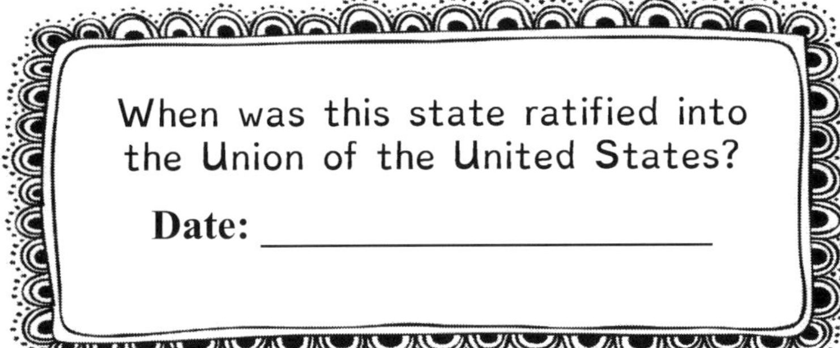

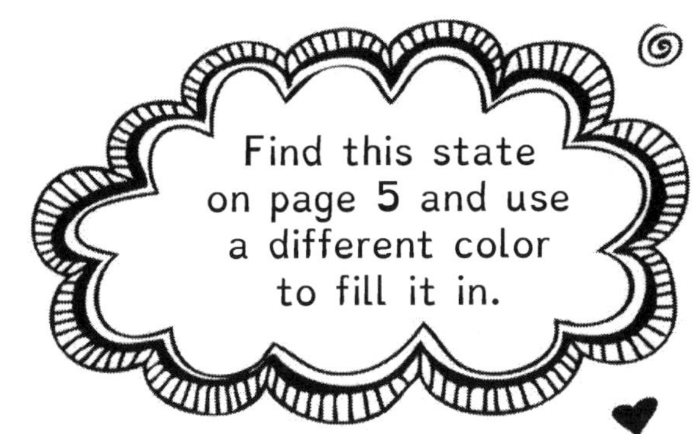

CREATIVE WRITING

In the space below, write a poem, short story, or a unique history tid-bit about the state flower. If this flower is in your state, and in bloom, try taping one to this page and press it in the book!

____

____

____

____

____

____

____

Which country did this flower originate?

____

List the different colors of this flower:

____

____

____

List the sources you used to research this flower:

Books: ____

____

Websites: ____

____

Other sources: ____

____

CREATIVE ARTS

Fill in the missing parts. Write the name of each flower from this section:

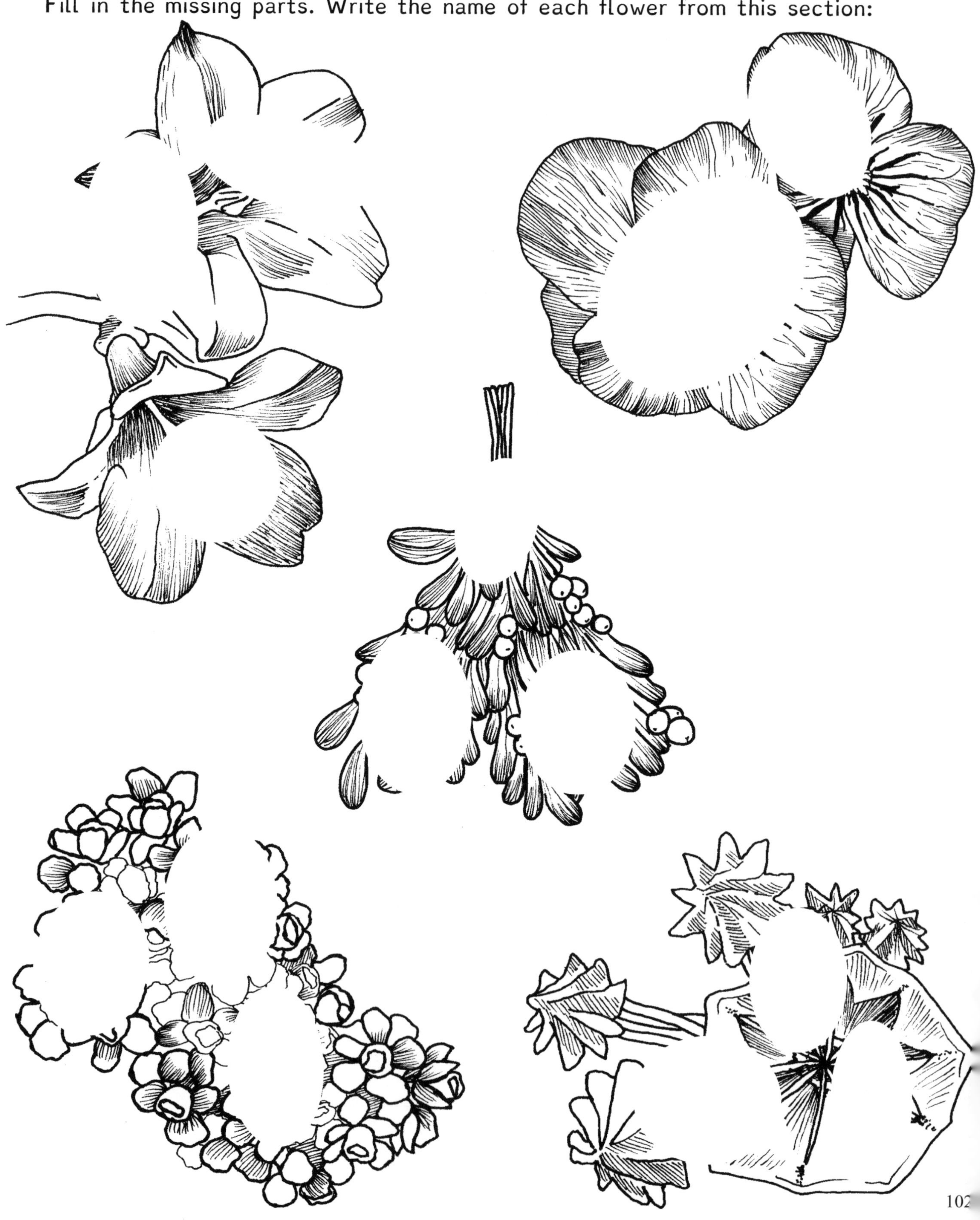

CREATIVE ARTS

Draw your favorite flower from this section. Use your imagination to draw the flower in its natural habitat. Add a house, forest, or animals!

SOUTH DAKOTA

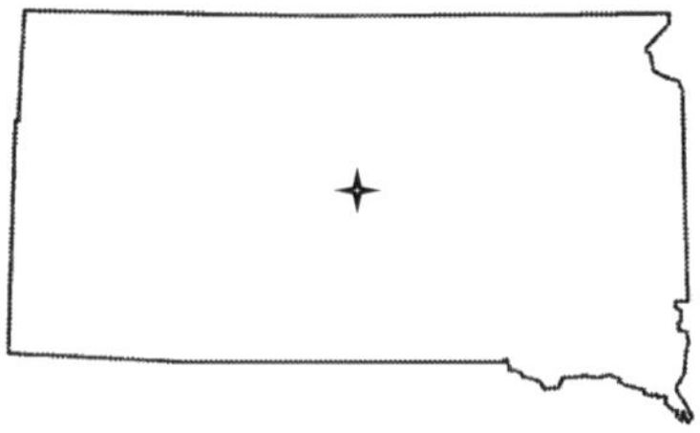

The state flower is:

American Pasque Flower

Find the botanical name: ____________________

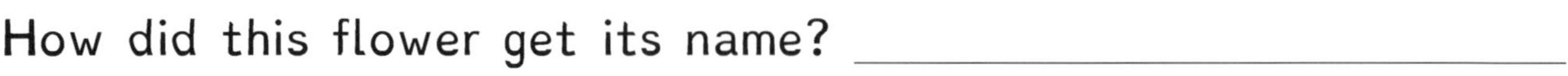

How did this flower get its name? ______________________________

____

Is this flower an annual or perennial? __________________

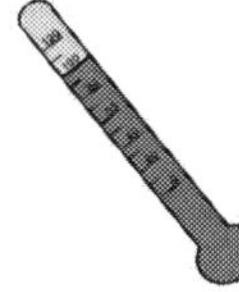

What range in temperature is best for this flower?

High: ___________ Low: _____________

How many hours of daily sunlight are needed for this flower? _____

Does this flower grow best in high or low altitude? ____________

List the type(s) of soil needed to grow the state flower: _________

____

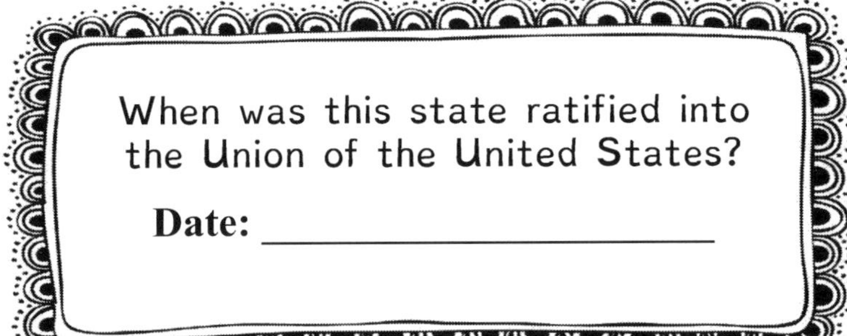

CREATIVE WRITING

In the space below, write a poem, short story, or a unique history tid-bit about the state flower. If this flower is in your state, and in bloom, try taping one to this page and press it in the book!

____

____

____

____

____

____

____

Which country did this flower originate?

____

List the different colors of this flower:

____

____

____

List the sources you used to research this flower:

Books: _______________________________________

____

Websites: _______________________________________

____

Other sources: _______________________________________

____

TENNESSEE

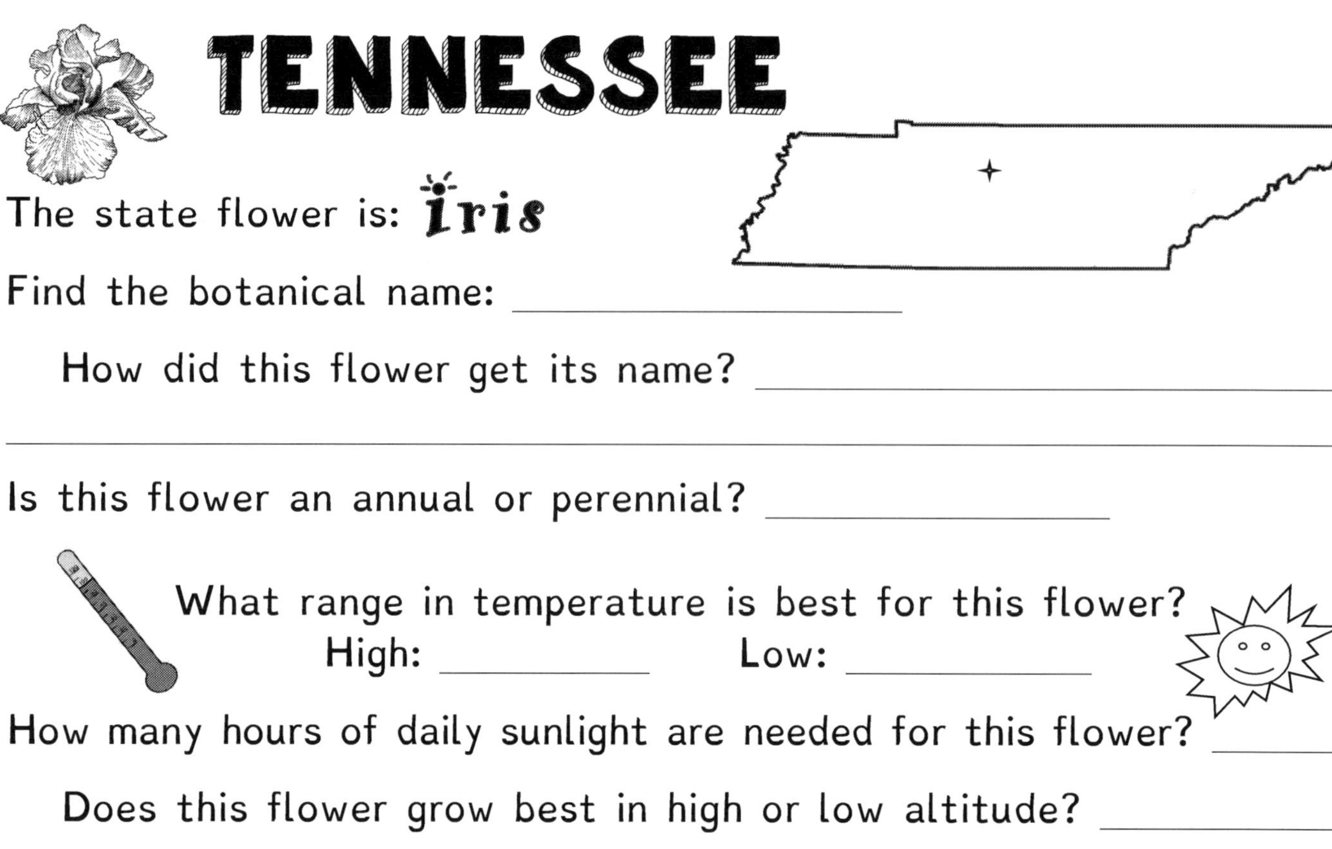

The state flower is: **Iris**

Find the botanical name: ____________________

How did this flower get its name? ______________________________

____

Is this flower an annual or perennial? __________________

What range in temperature is best for this flower?
High: __________ Low: ____________

How many hours of daily sunlight are needed for this flower? ______

Does this flower grow best in high or low altitude? ____________

List the type(s) of soil needed to grow the state flower: _________

____

Interesting fact: Greeneville, Tennessee is home to the annual Iris Festival.

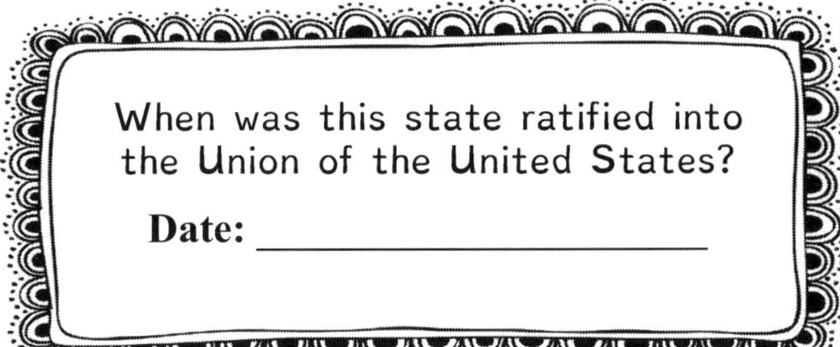

CREATIVE WRITING

In the space below, write a poem, short story, or a unique history tid-bit about the state flower. If this flower is in your state, and in bloom, try taping one to this page and press it in the book!

____

____

____

____

____

____

____

Which country did this flower originate?

____

List the different colors of this flower:

____

____

____

List the sources you used to research this flower:

Books: ____

____

Websites: ____

____

Other sources: ____

____

The state flower is: Bluebonnet

Find the botanical name: ____________________

How did this flower get its name? ____________________

____

Is this flower an annual or perennial? ________________

What range in temperature is best for this flower?
High: __________ Low: ____________

How many hours of daily sunlight are needed for this flower? ______

Does this flower grow best in high or low altitude? ___________

List the type(s) of soil needed to grow the state flower: ________

____

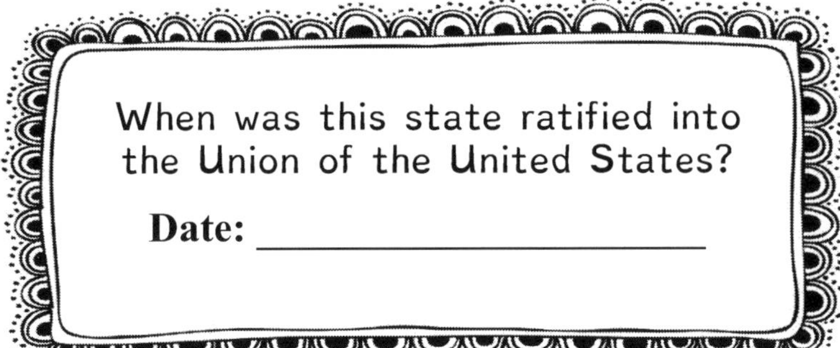

CREATIVE WRITING

In the space below, write a poem, short story, or a unique history tid-bit about the state flower. If this flower is in your state, and in bloom, try taping one to this page and press it in the book!

____

____

____

____

____

____

____

Which country did this flower originate?

____

List the different colors of this flower:

____

____

____

List the sources you used to research this flower:

Books: ______________________________________

____

Websites: ____________________________________

____

Other sources: ________________________________

____

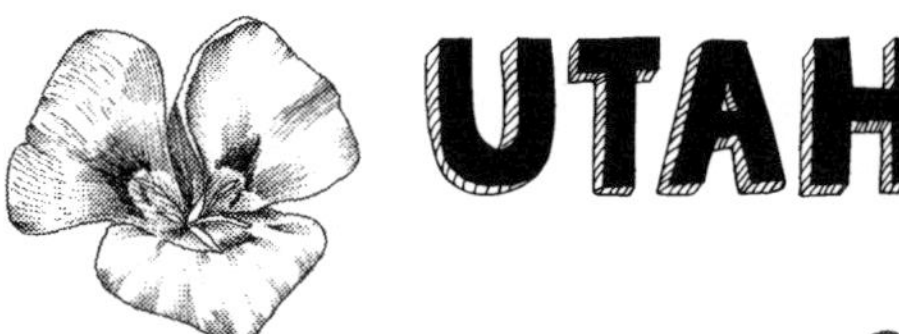

UTAH

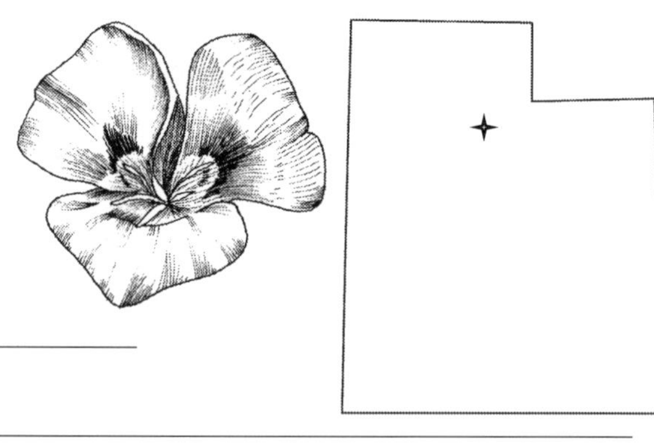

The state flower is: Sego Lily

Find the botanical name: ____________________

How did this flower get its name? ______________________________

____

Is this flower an annual or perennial? __________________

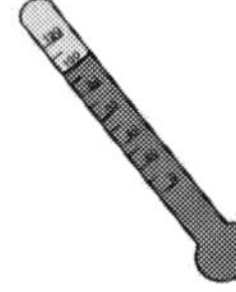

What range in temperature is best for this flower?

High: ___________ Low: _____________

How many hours of daily sunlight are needed for this flower? _____

Does this flower grow best in high or low altitude? ____________

List the type(s) of soil needed to grow the state flower: _________

____

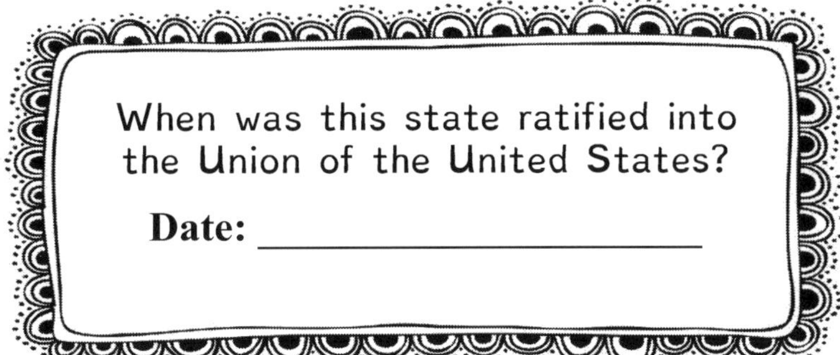

CREATIVE WRITING

In the space below, write a poem, short story, or a unique history tid-bit about the state flower. If this flower is in your state, and in bloom, try taping one to this page and press it in the book!

Which country did this flower originate?

____

List the different colors of this flower:

____

____

____

List the sources you used to research this flower:

Books: ______________________

Websites: ______________________

Other sources: ______________________

VERMONT

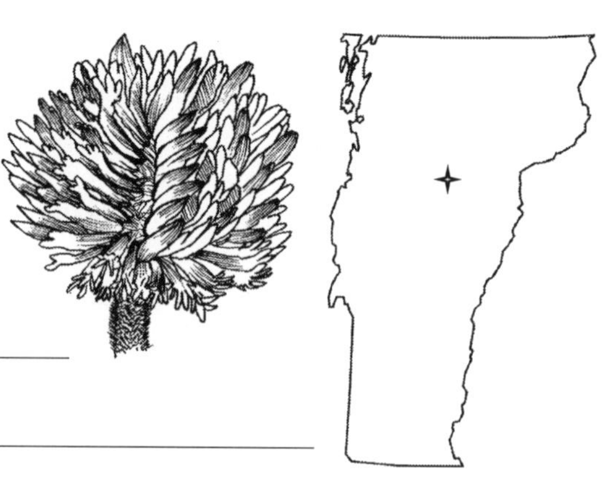

The state flower is: **Red Clover**

Find the botanical name: ____________________

How did this flower get its name? ____________________

____

Is this flower an annual or perennial? ____________________

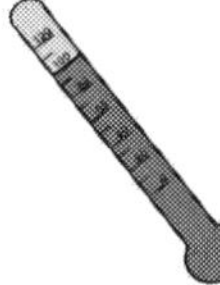

What range in temperature is best for this flower?
High: __________ Low: __________

How many hours of daily sunlight are needed for this flower? ______

Does this flower grow best in high or low altitude? __________

List the type(s) of soil needed to grow the state flower: ________

____

Fun fact:
The red clover is a favorite food of bovine!

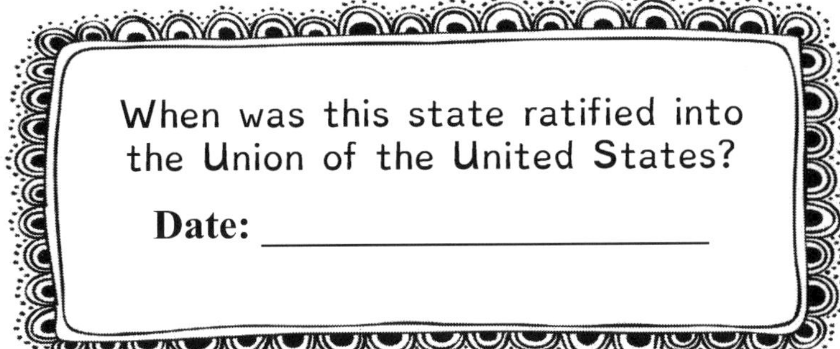

CREATIVE WRITING

In the space below, write a poem, short story, or a unique history tid-bit about the state flower. If this flower is in your state, and in bloom, try taping one to this page and press it in the book!

____

____

____

____

____

____

____

Which country did this flower originate?

____

List the different colors of this flower:

____

____

____

List the sources you used to research this flower:

Books: ____

____

Websites: ______________________________________

____

Other sources: ___________________________________

____

CREATIVE ARTS

Fill in the missing parts. Write the name of each flower from this section:

CREATIVE ARTS

Draw your favorite flower from this section. Use your imagination to draw the flower in its natural habitat. Add a house, forest, or animals!

VIRGINIA

The state flower is:

American Dogwood

Find the botanical name: ____________________

How did this flower get its name? ______________________________

____

Is this flower an annual or perennial? __________________

What range in temperature is best for this flower?

High: __________ Low: ____________

How many hours of daily sunlight are needed for this flower? ______

Does this flower grow best in high or low altitude? ______

List the type(s) of soil needed to grow the state flower: _________

____

Which other state declared Dogwood as their state flower?

____

What is the Virginia state tree?

____

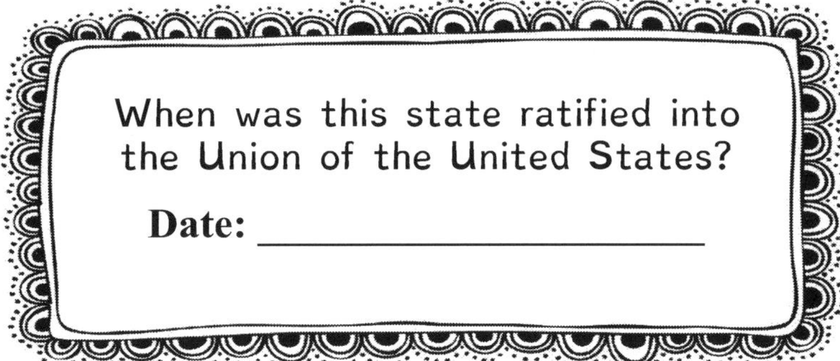

CREATIVE WRITING

In the space below, write a poem, short story, or a unique history tid-bit about the state flower. If this flower is in your state, and in bloom, try taping one to this page and press it in the book!

____

____

____

____

____

____

____

Which country did this flower originate?

____

List the different colors of this flower:

____

____

____

List the sources you used to research this flower:

Books: ____

____

Websites: ____

____

Other sources: ____

____

WASHINGTON

The state flower is:

Coast Rhododendron

Find the botanical name: ____________________

How did this flower get its name? ______________________________

Is this flower an annual or perennial? __________________

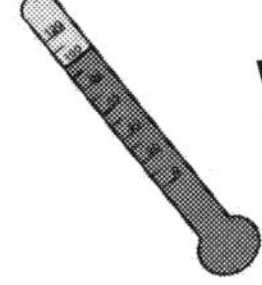

What range in temperature is best for this flower?

High: ___________ Low: ____________

How many hours of daily sunlight are needed for this flower? ______

Does this flower grow best in high or low altitude? __________

List the type(s) of soil needed to grow the state flower: ________

____

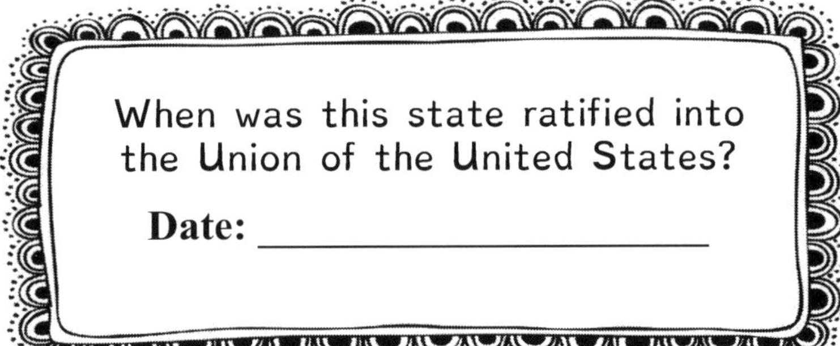

CREATIVE WRITING

In the space below, write a poem, short story, or a unique history tid-bit about the state flower. If this flower is in your state, and in bloom, try taping one to this page and press it in the book!

____

____

____

____

____

____

____

Which country did this flower originate?

____

List the different colors of this flower:

____

____

____

List the sources you used to research this flower:

Books: ____

____

Websites: ____

____

Other sources: ____

____

WEST VIRGINIA

The state flower is: **Rhododendron**

Find the botanical name: ______________

How did this flower get its name? ______________________

____

Is this flower an annual or perennial? ____________

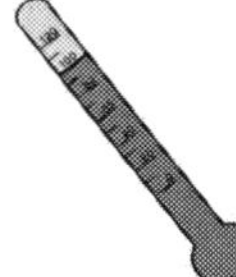

What range in temperature is best for this flower?
High: ________ Low: ________

How many hours of daily sunlight are needed for this flower? ______

Does this flower grow best in high or low altitude? ______

List the type(s) of soil needed to grow the state flower: ______

____

Describe the difference between a rhododendron and a coast rhododendron:

____

____

____

____

____

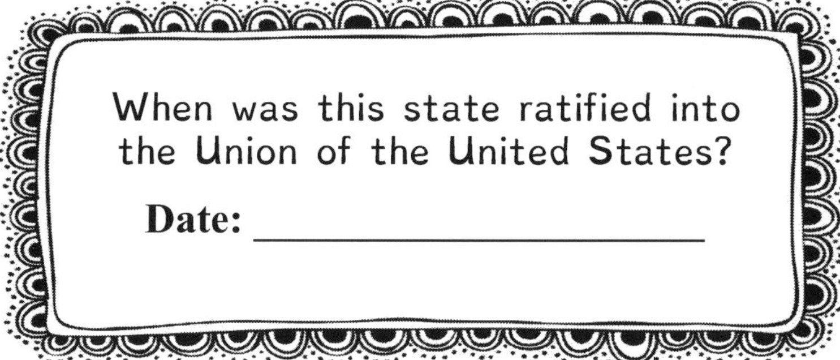

CREATIVE WRITING

In the space below, write a poem, short story, or a unique history tid-bit about the state flower. If this flower is in your state, and in bloom, try taping one to this page and press it in the book!

____

____

____

____

____

____

____

Which country did this flower originate?

____

List the different colors of this flower:

____

____

____

List the sources you used to research this flower:

Books: ____

____

Websites: ____

____

Other sources: ____

____

WISCONSIN

The state flower is: **Wood Violet**

Find the botanical name: ____________________

How did this flower get its name? ______________________________

____

Is this flower an annual or perennial? __________________

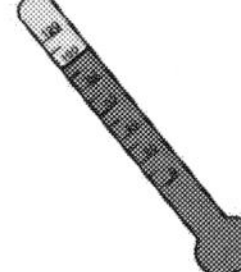

What range in temperature is best for this flower?

High: ___________ Low: _____________

How many hours of daily sunlight are needed for this flower? ______

Does this flower grow best in high or low altitude? ____________

List the type(s) of soil needed to grow the state flower: _________

____

Four states picked flowers in the Violet family for their state flower. Name the other three states:

____

____

____

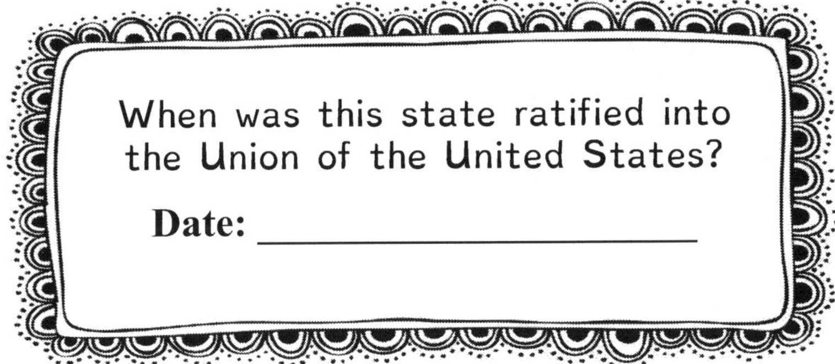

CREATIVE WRITING

In the space below, write a poem, short story, or a unique history tid-bit about the state flower. If this flower is in your state, and in bloom, try taping one to this page and press it in the book!

____

____

____

____

____

____

____

Which country did this flower originate?

____

List the different colors of this flower:

____

____

____

List the sources you used to research this flower:

Books: ____

____

Websites: ____

____

Other sources: ____

____

WYOMING

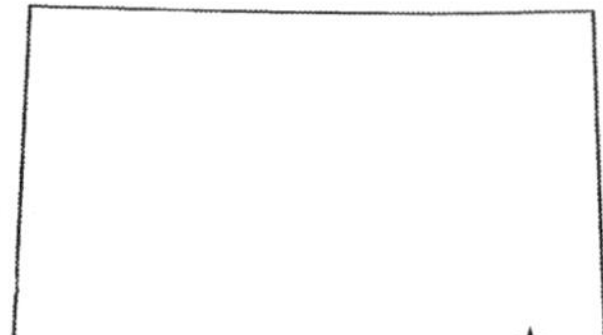

The state flower is: **Indian Paintbrush**

Find the botanical name: ____________________

How did this flower get its name? ______________________________

____

Is this flower an annual or perennial? __________________

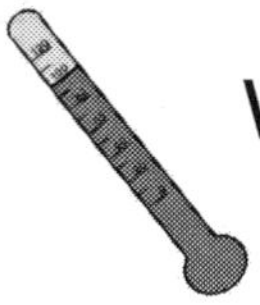

What range in temperature is best for this flower?
High: ___________ Low: _____________

How many hours of daily sunlight are needed for this flower? _____

Does this flower grow best in high or low altitude? __________

List the type(s) of soil needed to grow the state flower: _________

____

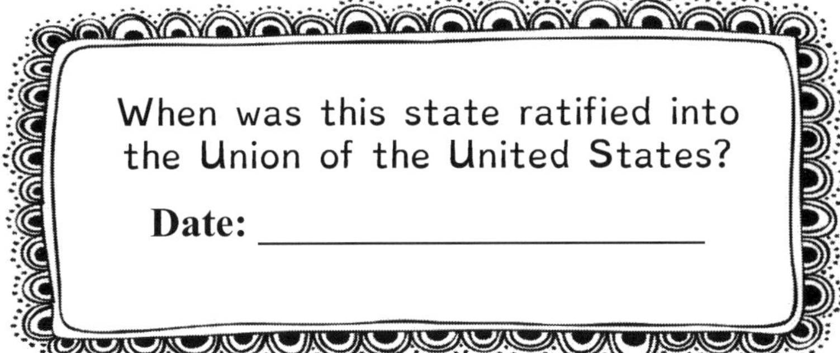

CREATIVE WRITING

In the space below, write a poem, short story, or a unique history tid-bit about the state flower. If this flower is in your state, and in bloom, try taping one to this page and press it in the book!

____

____

____

____

____

____

____

Which country did this flower originate?

____

List the different colors of this flower:

____

____

____

List the sources you used to research this flower:

Books: ____

____

Websites: ____

____

Other sources: ____

____

CREATIVE ARTS

Fill in the missing parts. Write the name of each flower from this section:

CREATIVE ARTS

Draw your favorite flower from this section. Use your imagination to draw the flower in its natural habitat. Add a house, forest, or animals!

FUNSCHOOLINGBOOKS.COM

Coffee

Made in the USA
Middletown, DE
01 March 2021